RESTORING HUMAN AGENCY TO EDUCATIONAL ADMINISTRATION:
Status and Strategies

HOW TO ORDER THIS BOOK

BY PHONE: 866-401-4337 or 717-290-1660, 9AM–5PM Eastern Time

BY FAX: 717-509-6100

BY MAIL: Order Department

ProActive Publications, Inc.

439 North Duke Street

Lancaster, PA 17601, U.S.A.

BY CREDIT CARD: American Express, VISA, MasterCard

BY WWW SITE: http://www.proactivepublications.com

RESTORING HUMAN AGENCY TO EDUCATIONAL ADMINISTRATION:
Status and Strategies

FENWICK ENGLISH
R. Wendell Eaves Senior Distinguished Professor of Educational Leadership
School of Education
University of North Carolina at Chapel Hill, North Carolina

and

ROSEMARY PAPA
Del and Jewell Lewis Endowed Chair for Educational Leadership
College of Education
Northern Arizona University Flagstaff, Arizona

Restoring Human Agency to Educational Administration

ProActive Publications
439 North Duke Street
Lancaster, Pennsylvania 17602-4967 U.S.A.

Printed in the United States of America
10 9 8 7 6 5 4 3 2 1

Main entry under title:
    Restoring Human Agency to Educational Administration: Status and Strategies

A ProActive Publications book
Bibliography: p.
Includes index p. 95

ISBN: 1-885432-50-X

Contents

Introduction

What Does It Mean to Restore Human Agency to Educational Administration and Leadership?

Before one "does" anything in educational leadership there is thinking, from deep thought to a momentary insight. We practice only what we know, but how do we know if we know enough? And how do we know if what we know is true? One bridge between thinking and doing leadership is provided by stories or narratives about beginnings and endings. Stories provide the fabric for both leaders and followers to come together. Stories also contribute meaning and hence value to human activities. The academic name given to stories is *theories*.

This book is about improving leadership practice. However it differs from the prevailing viewpoint as to how to accomplish that. We argue that practice is not improved by consolidating what is known, but by engaging in a pursuit of the unknown. It is only through improved and different research that we can accomplish the ambitious objective of being successful with all students in our schools. We maintain that improving school leadership is essentially learning how to think differently and more profoundly so as to connect theory and practice in novel ways. Yet, as will be demonstrated, the current national system of administrator accreditation, licensure, and dissertation research works *against* this essential professional pursuit by constructing, over the last half century, a discourse that reveals only a half face for understanding and improving practice.

After an explanation of what it means to restore human agency to educational administration and leadership, originally delivered as the 2009 Walter Cocking Lecture at the National Council of Professors of Educational Administration in San Antonio, Texas, Rosemary Papa and Fenwick English take a critical look at the quality of dissertation research across the field of education administration. The dissertation is the recognized capstone of a potential leader's ability to engage in rigorous and creative thinking about practice. This book analyzes a purposive sampling of dissertation research from 2006 to 2008 and shows there is much work to be done to improve the caliber of thinking and research in the field.

Finally, the distance between pursuing the unknown, the true role of the university in advancing professional knowledge, and the practice of the known as it is demonstrated in the doing of leadership, must be re-harmonized as current trends have diminished the role and respect for research and have vocationalized university preparation. Developments of this sort will stunt the long-term growth of the education administration profession and stifle its ability to exercise more effective leadership in schools in the 21st century.

We believe significant research that will advance our field comes with a thorough grasp of the history of its intellectual and conceptual development, as well as with an understanding how such evolution continues to shape our perceptions of the relationship between practice and theory. We also believe our field is too insular and narrow, especially in its locating of leadership within the social sciences. The key to a better future is to expand our research practices so that our lens is more inclusive. In short, leadership is a total package between the human exterior and interior. A better understanding of the interior or what some scholars have called "the subjective" is required for the preparation of leaders in all aspects of being a complete person. That is what we mean by restoring *human agency*. We want to recognize and thank our many friends and colleagues at UCEA and NCPEA for their support over the years. Your continued trust and good will are essential to our efforts to advance the conversation initiated by the publication of this book.

The Restoration of Human Agency in Educational Administration/Leadership Theory, Research, and Practice

The 2009 Walter Cocking Lecture of NCPEA
FENWICK W. ENGLISH

Introduction

Part 1 of the book comprises the 2009 Cocking Invitational Lecture for the annual conference of the National Council of Professors of Educational Administration. NCPEA was established in 1947 and has as one of its major objectives "to promote the application of theory and research in the field to the practice of educational administration" (Creighton, 2006, p. 691).

My initial NCPEA meeting occurred in 1977 in Eugene, Oregon, where I heard my first Cocking Lecture. At the time I had never heard of Walter Cocking. It was only after some time I learned he was a former teacher, principal and superintendent, earned his doctorate at TC Columbia and became a professor of educational administration at Vanderbilt. He served as the Tennessee State Commissioner of Education and later as Dean of the School of Education at the University of Georgia, from which he was fired for his support of integrated schools.

He went on to serve in high-level positions in the federal government and in 1947, at the AASA conference in Atlantic City, he helped found the National Council of Professors of Educational Administration. As the author of influential textbooks in our field, Cocking wrote about the organization and establishment of educational systems and educational practices in American schools (Grady, 2006, 157–8). With his contributions in mind I am honored to have been asked to give the Cocking Lecture at NCPEA in 2009.

1

I'd like to think that given Walter Cocking's life in educational admin-istration and his dismissal as dean at the University of Georgia for push-ing what today would be called an agenda of social justice, he was not only a man of principle, but one who raised important issues even when they might be professionally risky and highly unpopular. It is within this rich legacy that I want to address you today. My remarks are not only for professors, but also for thoughtful practitioners who share concerns about the state of knowledge in our field, and who are confronting daily the demands for improvements in practice to make equal and excellent education a reality for all children.

There is an intimate connection between the work of the university and educational leadership practice, though that connection has often been ob-scure at times and even contentious. I view with alarm the current trends and their impact on the role of the university in the overall picture of im-proving school leadership practice. I do not believe, nor do I find any evi-dence from our profession or the history of other applied professions, that the consolidation of existing practices into simplistic doctrine, which is subsequently enforced by state and accreditation agencies, is healthy in the short term for the advancement of leadership in the schools. Consolidation of this type is also not conducive to the long-term role of the university in advancing the boundaries of conceptual and theoretical thought.

I am reminded of the work of Imre Lakatos (1999), who cogently ob-served a theory-practice gap exists when the practices in a field cannot be predicted by the theories in use in the field. He calls the situation where a research program's theoretical base is behind practice, "regressive". When the theoretical content of a research program anticipates and pre-dicts problems of practice and its effects, it is "progressive."

We have in education administration a mostly regressive situation, and it won't be solved by longer internships in the field or by tweaking the ISLLC standards or forcing university professors to become voca-tional teachers of de-skilled curricula. If anything, these movements are counter-productive to where we must go. I will argue that employing Lakatos' (1999) idea of "theoretical pluralism" is a powerful antidote to the current situation, and I will also try to illustrate the obstacles and bar-riers to its development and implementation. I would like to imagine that if Walter Cocking were alive today he would approve. So let us begin.

Where Are We Now? Locating the Present: A Period of Scholasticism, Standardization and Stagnation

As a scholar, I am one of a small number who are chiefly interested in the currents of educational theory and conceptual thought that influence and sustain our field (see Gunter, 2006). I'm interested in how ideas locate themselves and become part of practice. It is clear that a field grows from its theories and not from its practices, especially an applied field such as educational administration.

James LeFanu (1999) has shown rather conclusively that in medicine, another and older applied professional field to which we are often compared, great breakthroughs in practice were attained not by consolidating them in hopes of finding a "best practice," but when the theory base changed in which practice itself was subsequently re-defined. In fact, the consolidations of the great physician of antiquity, Galen (c. 130–c.200), of medical practice in his time greatly inhibited the development of modern medicine for over one thousand years because of the fundamental errors on which his condensations were based (Porter, 1999, pp. 73–82).

John Dewey (1963) expressed the problem succinctly when he observed that experience obtained without the benefit of being placed within a larger plan [theory] was "wholly in the air" (p. 28). In a section of the 1904 National Society for the Scientific Study of Education in 1904, Dewey (1964) also stressed the importance of acquiring and controlling "the intellectual methods required for personal and independent mastery of practical skill, rather than at turning out at once masters of the craft" (p. 315). However, in the construction of the standards for those entering our field we have forgotten the advice Dewey proffered over one hundred years ago and we have embraced the consolidation and enshrinement of craft knowledge as a substitute (see Blumberg, 1989).

Collins (1998) has examined the larger intellectual currents in philosophy from the Chinese philosophers, 400–200 B.C.E. through the phenomenologists and existentialists, 1865–1965. What he notes is that an intellectual field becomes stagnant when its principle works are compendiums and anthologies, when the major scholars are more concerned with codifying and collecting and "worshipping exalted texts from the past which are regarded as containing the completion of all wisdom" (p. 31). This outlook is known as *scholasticism* when it dominates an intellectual period, "Eminence . . . goes to those persons who make themselves the most impressive guardians of the classics" (p. 31). This is the situation in educational administration. Scholasticism can be necessary as a way to build a "knowledge base," which is required for standardization. However, scholasticism is a more prevalent and pervasive perspective.

In a scientific field a similar stagnancy shows itself when knowledge becomes "fixed" (as in a knowledge base). Such stagnancy is contrasted to creating more robust theories and narratives. Stagnancy can occur when we are more concerned with research rigor than with research vibrancy, and when we are more interested in our political weight than our epistemological trajectory. I find intellectual recidivism in the phrase, "the belief that better theories will be the savior of educational practice . . . is a little like the case for cold fusion" (Murphy, 1999, p. 48). Murphy's comment is rebutted by Edward Deming who said that "experience alone, without theory, teaches management nothing about what to do to improve quality and competitive position, nor how to do it. . . . Experience will answer a question and a question comes from theory" (p. 19). Pierre Bourdieu (1998) spoke about the neoliberals and their use of theory in the culture wars and observed:

> One of the theoretical and practical errors of many theories . . . has been the failure to take account of the power of theory. We must no longer make that mistake. We are dealing with opponents who are armed with theories and I think they need to be fought with intellectual and cultural weapons (p. 53–4).

Collins (1998) makes it clear that when "a community is oriented toward innovation, great truths are not so much an advantage as an obstacle" (p. 32). What philosophical history demonstrates, according to Collins (1998), is that "for an intellectual community to be in a great creative age, it must be making great discoveries and also overturning them, and not just once, but over and again" (p. 32).

It is my position that our field is in the intellectual mode of scholasticism about its past in order to create political stability and to sustain the (mistaken) belief that retrenchment will exalt its status on the larger political landscape and enhance the relative position of those who are part of the standardization/scholasticism process. Although I have been a frequent critic of the standardization and scholasticism of our field (English 1997; 2002; 2003, 2006), I too have been part of this process (English, 2009), and so this presentation is offered not as blame or finger pointing, but rather as an effort to understand where we are, what we have done, and what we need to do to produce a more innovative and creative culture for improved research and practice.

It ought to be clear that the term "knowledge base" connotes the construction of a stable platform upon which to engage in other activities believed to be part of a profession. I find the idea epistemologically indefensible. Endorsing a knowledge base, similar to standardizing linguistic usage, requires a political effort, since power is needed to freeze language development at a particular place in its natural continuum of usage. To me the idea of freezing professional development of our field is unwise, since within our current state there is not only much we do not know, but much we have not been able to improve.

I can't imagine freezing medical practice at its current state where according to Emanuel (2006) "on the average, patients receive only 55 percent of proven primary-care interventions . . . [and] hundreds of thousands, if not millions, of patients receive unnecessary treatments" (p. B12) and I am reminded of the folly of the former Commissioner of the U.S. Patent Office who declared in 1899 that "Everything that can be invented has been invented" (The Quotations Page, 2009). Do we really believe that existing leadership practice is as good as it is ever going to get and contains no flaws?

The signs of a field's vibrancy are exhibited not by the collections of research already completed, but in the debates and contestation about ideas and schools of thought in which practice is defined. I see very little of that in our field. I find it revealing that none of the texts about educational leadership, which are about or linked to the ISLLC-ELCC standards, acknowledge what the standards miss or fail to include. There are no discussions about the presuppositions on which they are based and no acknowledgement of the points of tension and conflict they engendered in their development (see Hessel and Holloway, 2002; Shipman, Queen and Peel, 2007; Hanson, 2009; Razik and Swanson, 2010). The standards are presented ahistorically and are replete with power/knowledge suppositions that comprise a master regulatory narrative (a metanarrative as in Cherryholmes,1988) grounded in efficiency. However, as Usher and Edwards (1966) note, "efficiency has no end" but is a teleology, true by definition and self-contained (p. 166).

The national standards' presuppositions are rarely, if ever, explicated by their proponents or as Devitt and Sterelny (1987) explain:

> One cannot theorize about anything, least of all language, without implicit commitment to a view of the world. As a result, attempts to eliminate metaphysics lead not to its elimination but to its mystification; the philosopher has to hide or deny his own metaphysical assumptions (p. 190).

One is left with the impression that the proponents either don't know the full depth of their own assumptions and world views, which are deeply hegemonic of the status quo, or that they simply don't care about them or fully reveal them. The latter case is certainly more sinister than the former, though the result may be the same in stifling serious efforts to improve practice through more creative theorizing or developing alternative approaches to the dominant discursive perspectives.

By denying or denigrating the importance of debating the presuppositions of the practices which have been reified in the standards, those in power retain their privileges to control them without serious challenge to their hegemony. For me it amounts to saying, "If we already know everything we need to know about leading schools, there is no need to look further except to implement with greater fidelity the current knowledge base." There simply is no objective way of supporting such a stance with logic or evidence. To do so one would have to find a way of showing that the current state of knowledge was completely adequate for resolving all of the outstanding issues of education in our society. Such evidence simply does not exist, though the silence of the proponents is disturbing since they don't admit to any imperfections. Paul Feyerabend (1993) cautioned, ". . . the belief in a unique set of standards that has always led to success and will always lead to success is nothing but a chimera" (p. 160).

The late Joe Rost (1991) summarized the last fifty years of work in which educational leadership has been subsumed in the social sciences with its historical roots in the arts and humanities erased or ignored, is instructive:

> Leadership studies as an academic discipline need to come out of the woodwork of management science in all of its guises . . . and out of such disciplines as social psychology, political science and sociology (p.182).

A Portrait of The Half Face of Leadership That Dominates Our Mindscapes and Our Work

It will be my line of argument that human agency, the idea that an individual human being is a purposive moral agent and can act within or without the social structures in ways which are "rooted in a value system and [with] a sense of personal identity," (Bandura, 2001, p. 14) remains in the shadows of the face of leadership in the standards we have adopted in preparing leaders, in the dominant modes we have come to in conducting the discourse about leadership, and in the principle ways we engage in research about it. We continue to be in thrall to business, economic and market theories, in which as Bourdieu (1998) has observed, we have traded "things of logic for the logic of things" (p. 101). That dependence has begun to seriously erode the role of the university in constructing the theoretical basis of improving practice, and is moving preparation programs to little more than vocational trade craft apprenticeships. John Dewey (1929) observed that such an approach is dominated by persons who simply want to know "how to do things with the maximum prospect of success. Put baldly, they want recipes" (p. 15).

I also believe that this dominant half-face of leadership erodes our capacity to change schools deeply and to adjust the present arc of the societal function of schools, which now serve as the social agents of

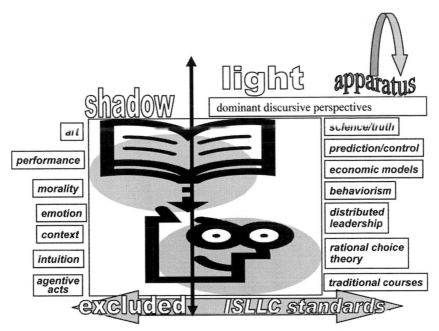

FIGURE 1 A Bricolage of Two Sides of Leadership.

reproduction of inequities and social/economic injustices (see Bourdieu and Passeron, 2000).

To try and unpack some of the threads of my argument into a more coherent presentation, I want to begin by showing Figure 1. Here I present a bricolage of the two sides of the face of leadership. A bricolage is a construction of something using what is at hand so the elements shown on either side of the face are not equal. However each side constitutes what Bourdieu (2001) has called an *epistemocratic justification* (p. 34).

The right side is the dominant ideological side, the side which is most visible and most in currency at the present time. The left side is the subordinate side, the one in the shadows, the one that has been there even longer than the right side, but which is considered inferior in any number of ways, largely because the context of our times has succeeded in placing it in a subordinated position because it isn't "scientific" or "rigorous" by some standards of research and does not lend itself easily, if at all, to licensure standardization and scoring rubrics used by the ISLLA (Interstate School Leaders Licensure Assessment) or to methods such as controlled field trials (see English, 2007).

The long journey of our field towards professional standards as recounted by Hoyle (2006) Murphy (2005) and English (2004, 2008) among others, rests on centering some ideological/epistemological perspectives and de-centering and de-legitimizing others. By ideology I do not mean doctrine that in the popular mind is "pseudo-science," but a series of statements about things (some of which may be true and some false) that rest on predispositions, which are either unstated or unknown to those proposing them (see Watt, 1994, p. 185).

The centering process by which the national standards were legitimized was not based solely on research evidence, of which there is precious little. And, what is available is hardly unequivocal (see Murphy, 2005 for an explication). What the proponents of the national standards engaged in was the construction of a platform to anchor a political apparatus, exercising control via policing (accreditation) inherent in the power to give examinations, provide licensure, and deny admission to positions of power by those already in power under an umbrella of "wisdom of the field" consensus, something which has been attacked by right wing critics as a failed monopoly (see Hess, 2004; Finn, 1991). What is really at stake is the control of the profession and the existing power of the prevailing political/professional apparatus (Kowalski, 2004; English, 2004).

Understanding the Dominant Ideological Face: Foucault's *Apparatus*

By *apparatus* is meant here Michel Foucault's (1980) notion that there is an interlocking fabric of agencies connected by common interests and agendas within a common *discourse*. A *discourse* consists of areas, occupations, roles, customs, rules, and traditions that center conversation, both oral and written. The function of a discourse is normative; that is, it serves to enforce and reinforce certain ways of thinking, speaking and acting. As Fairclough (1992) explains, a discourse constructs what it describes and then reproduces it (p. 41). Fairclough (1992) elaborates:

> Discourse as a political practice establishes, sustains and changes power relations, and the collective entities (classes, blocs, communities, groups) between which power relations obtain. Discourse as an ideological practice constitutes, naturalizes, sustains and changes significations of the world from diverse positions in power relations (p. 67).

When agencies, institutions, and associations become linked and engage in expressing and enforcing their common agenda within a discourse, a regime of truth is established. Authorities within a *regime of truth* can at this point function to repress, discourage and inhibit alternative discourses or viewpoints. Within this context "truth" is produced and becomes a commodity. Foucault adds:

> 'Truth' is centered on the form of scientific discourse and the institutions which produce it; it is subject to constant economic and political incitement (the demand for truth, as much for economic production as for political power); it is the object, under diverse forms of immense diffusion and consumption (circulating through apparatuses of education and information whose extent is relatively broad in the social body . . . ; it is produced and transmitted under the control, dominant if not exclusive, of a few great political and economic apparatuses (university, army, writing, media) (Foucault, 1980, 131–32).

Those functioning within the *apparatus* are given certain privileges, among them the right to speak and to question things. Foucault (1972) brings this home by asking "Who is speaking? Who among the totality of speaking individuals, is accorded the right to use this sort of language?" (p. 50). From this perspective it becomes clear that not all individuals are accorded the same credibility in expressing satisfaction or dissatisfaction with the existing state of affairs. Within the realm of educational leadership and administration, external critics are roped off for a variety of reasons (see Kowalski, 2004).

This is not always negative. Nonetheless, the normative process works both ways by excluding viewpoints it considers harmful. In educational leadership, one can cite the Broad Foundation's and Thomas B. Fordham Institute's (2003) anonymous attack on leadership programs in schools of education, and a later report by Arthur Levine (2005), which among other things advocated replacing the Ed.D. with an MBA. But a regime of truth also works to repress changes which come to be viewed as positive, such as reacting very negatively to Thomas B. Greenfield's (1988) criticisms regarding the dominance of organizational theory and positivistic science in educational leadership, which sparked the famous *Greenfield/Griffiths Debate* (Kendell & Byrne, 1977). In that debate Greenfield (1988) wrote:

> Positivistic science cannot derive a value from a fact or even recognize values as real, we have a science of administration which can deal only with facts and which does so by eliminating from its consideration all human passion, weakness, strength, conviction, hope, pity, frailty, altruism, courage, vice, and virtue (p. 137).

Greenfield's criticisms were met with a firestorm of opposition because he had penetrated to the ideological core, the university anchor of the prevailing *apparatus*. Other serious debates in educational leadership would occur later over qualitative research, critical theory and critical race theory, as well as postmodernism (Willower, 1998; English, 1998).

The reason even beneficial changes are often stoutly resisted has been identified by Barrows Dunham (1964):

> Human organizations are founded and built by human beings, and their ideologies have precisely the same human source. It follows that into the ideologies of organizations there creep errors, which may on occasion be gross. Once these errors embed themselves in doctrine they are beyond the reach of easy correction. They have become part of the source of unity. Their removal is not a mere scientific adjustment, but a dislocation of the corporate body (pp. 17–18).

Dunham adds that those who stay within human organizations and do not question such errors are defenders of the prevailing orthodoxy, while those who question them are always heretics. At the base of such actions and reactions lies the unity of the organization and in the case of an *apparatus* its political power to retain control of the functions or services within its purview.

The dominant side of the face of educational leadership in Figure 1 is made up of certain views of the nature of science, which if not positivistic are certainly empirical and contain all the earmarks of empirical inquiry. The linkage between empirical science, the need for prediction and control, the use of economic models, the widespread application of rational choice theory across the full spectrum of course work and assignments in educational administration, including the notion of distributed leadership, is packaged with a behavioral view of the individual leader and reflected in traditional course work in most educational leadership programs. This collection of perspectives comprises what Foucault (1972) has called "a field of presence," which signifies a general acceptance within a discourse that the statements within it should be accepted because they possess "experimental verification, logical validation, mere repetition . . . [and] are justified by tradition and authority, commentary" (p. 57).

I should note that I have placed distributed leadership on this side because while authority and sometimes accountability are *dispersed* formally or informally across a wide range of bureaucratic roles and/or units (see Gronn, 2003), the concept fits conveniently into organizational hierarchy and all of the attendant sociological theories of organization and decisional rationality which continue to efface human agency in educational systems.

The dispersion of responsibility and/or accountability can be highly impersonal even though in another sense it is more democratic. Whether or not such dispersions are truly democratic is a matter of discernment regarding the epistemocratic presuppositions held and whether a rationalist perspective is ever subjected to scrutiny. Democracy is not possible if those involved have no way of subjecting even the rationalist perspective to critical review (see Woods, 2005, p. 50).

Understanding the Subordinate/Shadow Side of Educational Leadership

The subordinated side of leadership in our work involves performance as an art form (English, 2008, 2008b) and the legitimate recognition of emotion and culture in the actual practice of leadership (Bolton & English, 2009). Lumby and English (2009) see leadership "as a form of ritualized mythic performance" where becoming an educational leader is "fundamentally the creation of a performance, a fabrication, the crafting and enactment of a ritualized role as in a theatre performance" (p. 103). Furthermore, art is part and parcel of moral behavior and hinges on Bandura's (2001) notion of agentive acts encompassing moral conduct (see Doscher and Normore, 2008).

Much of what comprises the bricolage on the shadow side of leadership has been cast into what Foucault (1972) has called "a field of memory," which is constituted by statements no longer accepted or discussed, and that consequently no longer define a "body of truth or a domain validity" (p. 58). My intention is to try and restore the shadow side, the "field of memory," to the "field of presence." How this side of the face of leadership, which is much older than the now dominant discursive perspective or light side in Figure 1, became supplanted by the latter is part of the historical abandonment of the long legacy of the arts and humanities in our field. The shadow side was pushed into the "field of memory" (Foucault, 1972, p. 57) under the onslaught of the pseudoscience of Taylorism, the rise of behaviorism and its empirical tenets that only experience and the observable count (see Bloomfield, 1933), social pressures for efficiency, and the need for academic legitimacy and territoriality on the part of the newly emerging departments of educational administration within the also emergent schools of education. These inchoate departments were highly insular and produced dissertations of "embarrassing narrowness" (Schaefer, 1990, p. 61), a situation that still exists and will be addressed in the second part of this book.

The shadow side of leadership was pushed further into the "field of memory" with the rise of the theory movement as exemplified in logical positivism in the social sciences and the work of early sociologists such as Robert Merton (1951) and Talcott Parsons (1966). Bolman and Deal's

(1991) frame theory represents the epitome of the sociological/organizational theory perspective in which all the frames as forms of structuralism erode human agency.

The National Apparatus for Educational Leadership

A depiction of the national Foucauldian apparatus in educational leadership is shown in Figure 2. It is based on descriptions by Hoyle (2006) and Shipman (2006) that the establishment of the ISLLC standards "were created by those most knowledgeable and *in control* of the field of educational administration in the United States at the time" (p. 524). A brief explanation may help the reader see the connections and relationships it depicts.

The following acronyms are used in Figure 2.

AASA—American Association of School Administrators
AERA—American Education Research Association
ASCD—Association for Supervision and Curriculum Development
CCSSO—Council of Chief State School Officers
ELCC—Educational Leaders Constituent Council

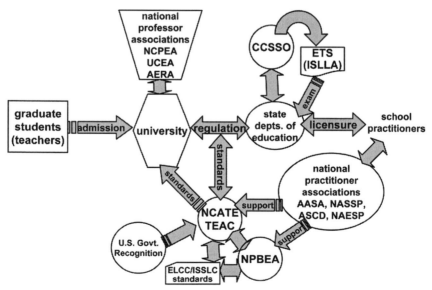

FIGURE 2 The National Apparatus for Educational Leadership.

ETS—Educational Testing Service
ISLLA—Interstate Leaders Licensure Assessment
ISLLC—Interstate School Leaders Licensure Consortium
NAESP—National Association of Elementary School Principals
NASSP—National Association of Secondary School Principals
NCATE—National Council for the Accreditation of Teacher Education
NCPEA—National Council of Professors of Educational Administration
NPBEA—National Policy Board for Educational Administration
TEAC—Teacher Education Accreditation Council
UCEA—University Council for Educational Administration

While NCPEA was founded in 1947 in cooperation with AASA (the American Association of School Administrators), NCATE (National Council for the Accreditation of Teacher Education) did not come into being until 1954. The university remains in a pivotal but very different role now than it did a half-century ago. At one time university professors were the dominant figures in defining the intellectual centers and margins of practice. With the rise of NCATE and its normative role in policing departments of educational administration and leadership as a part of the regulative review of colleges of education, and with practitioner associations supporting the accreditation process, national education associations in the United States now have a powerful voice in exercising hegemony over administrator preparation. When these forces were joined by chief state school officers and state departments of education in the establishment of the ISLLC standards through the CCSSO, the regulatory review process profoundly shifted the power in our field away from the university.

Unfortunately, the result has been a turning away from the need for and support of new conceptual and theoretical models the field so desperately needs to expand the range and content of practice. Instead what we are witnessing is the reification of existing notions of the methods of practice in a move embodying role de-skilling and the dumbing down of university course work in the accountability mechanisms required by NCATE. Simultaneously, we are in the midst of the rise of rival forms of preparation with on-line universities such as Capella, Walden and the University of Phoenix to name a few. And the on-line alternatives are all sanctioned by their use of the ISLLC-ELCC standards (see Hess and Kelly, 2005).

The repositioning of the sources of influence within the educational leadership apparatus around the creation and implementation of the ISLLC-ELCC standards (ISLLC = Interstate School Leaders Licensure Consortium, ELCC = Educational Leaders Consortium Council, see

Shipman, Queen & Peel, 2007) has also seen the balkanization of the cadre of professors involved with leadership preparation into those representing largely local and regional preparation institutions at the masters level, and those involved with preparing leaders at the doctoral level. The shift in the production of degrees has also been profound and is documented by Baker, Orr and Young (2007) and in the dissertations reviewed below in Part 2.

A really rich history of this profound transformation of our field surely needs to be written on a similar scale as Callahan's (1962) classic *Education and the Cult of Efficiency* for the first half of the last century, and Rakesh Khurana's (2007) history of the rise and transformation of schools of business and management practice in the last half of the same century. Although Tom Glass' (2004) book *The History of Educational Administration Viewed Through Its Textbooks* is a good start, we need more scholarly work in our field's conceptual and intellectual patterns to avoid the ahistoricism from which we have perennially suffered and through which human agency has been eroded or erased.

Jackie Blount (2008) also has expressed the view that "the field of educational leadership and administration generally lacks an overarching historical self-awareness" (p. 17) and that the scholarship in our field examines history in an insular and chronological way rather than researching "the scholars producing the work, the school administrators described by that work, or especially the larger social contexts in which the field has unfolded" (pp. 17–18).

My view of the existing educational leadership apparatus is that some form of it is inevitable. My criticism of it in our field is that it has largely worked to oversimplify the challenges we face, produce underprepared leaders, and to form a barrier to moving the field forward with its anti-intellectualism towards the necessity for theoretical alternatives through its preoccupation with control and its extreme utilization of job de-skilling as embodied in its adoption of the ISLLC-ELCC standards.

A similar kind of structure or apparatus exists in selecting business CEOs, despite exhortations about business not having licensure requirements as in education (see Hess, 2004). Khurana (2002) closely examined the practices of how corporations hired their CEOs and noted that, "While today's CEO labor market is defended as if it were a market in the classical sense, it is in reality nothing of the sort" (p. 186). Khurana (2002) explained "socially based categories of eligibility, the evaluations of investors and the media, and third-partner intermediaries (i.e., executive search firms) play a central role in controlling access to jobs and facilitating or hindering mobility" (pp. 186–7).

There is no truth outside an apparatus because there is no truth outside of its power. Foucault (1980) observed this when he said, "Truth is a thing of this world: it is produced only by virtue of multiple forms of constraint" (p. 131). Every society has a power apparatus which determines:

the types of discourse which it accepts and makes function as true; the mechanisms and instances which enable one to distinguish true and false statements, the means by which each is sanctioned; the techniques and procedures accorded value in the acquisition of truth; the status of those who are charged with saying what counts as true (Foucault, 1980, p. 131).

The apparatus in educational leadership represents Foucault's (1980) *power/knowledge* concept. Knowledge is never neutral. It is defined by its placement in hierarchies of power. It defines, produces and regulates what is the sanctioned discourse. I believe the current apparatus is extremely harmful to the long-term health and development of our discipline.

Finally, on this point the right wing think tank pundits have correctly identified the keystone in the extant apparatus as *licensure* because it is this legalistic process end product that results in the political power to regulate policy and practice in educational leadership (see Hess, 2004; 2008). It is interesting that the rationale for granting professional certificates, which began in 1925 in California, was adapted from business and that as Callahan (1962) noted, "The unfortunate aspect of this development was not the idea of certifying or controlling the men who would administer the public schools but the nature of the work they were forced to take" (p. 251).

While academia becomes more normative and even punitive with its sanctions, the political right's larger agenda of promoting free- market capitalism within the neo-liberal agenda has repeatedly stumbled over it (see DeMarris, 2006; O'Conner, 2007; Lather, 2009). As Ellen Willis (2005) trenchantly observed, "To a radical right that feels entitled to dominate not only government but all social institutions, the academy is a particular irritant" (p. B11). I now look at the role of the academy in this discussion.

The Conservative Intertextuality of the University

Figure 3 provides a closer look into the intertextual discursive practice of preparing school leaders in the United States at the doctoral level in a typical university setting. The concept of intertextuality is one that indicates that one text is related to another without regard to its author(s). The idea is that no author is necessary once human thought is placed on pa-

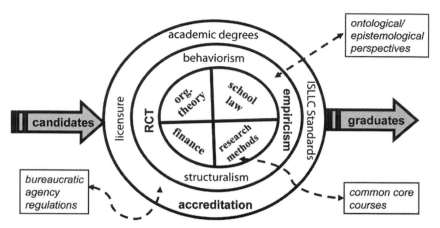

FIGURE 3 The University's Doctoral Discursive Intertextual Practice in Educational Administration.

per. No one person thinks alone and language has a life of its own and speaks through people (Foucault, 1972). "Discursive practice" means specific forms of speech and writing that adhere to certain relational rules that indicate "the roles and qualifications for the utterers of specific discourse, the mode of specification of their objects of knowledge, the conceptual frameworks for the derivation, formalization and systematization of utterances, and the strategic relations of conditioning and effect operating between discourses and other forms of social practice" (Foucault, 1980, p. 244).

Figure 3 shows how graduate students enter a doctoral intertextual practice in a typical university program in educational administration/leadership. While they take courses, of which some of the most common are shown in the center, they may be unaware of the enveloping epistemological perspectives of behaviorism, structuralism, empiricism and rational choice theory (RCT). Behaviorism is a perspective regarding psychology that limits a study of leaders to observable actions and eliminates "concepts of mind and consciousness" and tends to view "thinking and emotion as implicit behavior" (Wood, 1984, p. 50–1). Behaviorism underlies such management ideologies as scientific management, total quality management, and applied behavioral analysis (Blackbourn, 2006, pp. 70–73).

Structuralism is generally believed to have emanated from the work of Ferdinand Saussure, a Swiss linguist (Gadet, 1986). Within structuralism a word's meaning is only determined by the context of other words in which it is embedded. It has no meaning outside of its relationship to other words. Thus, in larger structures, one can only know what meaning there is by understanding the substructures, and their meaning can only be discerned "by inference and deduction from observed empirical data" (Allison, 1999, pp. 882–4).

RCT or rational choice theory is the dominant perspective in describing decision making in educational administration and includes mathematical models, game theory and models of economic decision rendering centered on competitive economic behavior (see Bolton & English, 2009).

Nowhere is the marriage between RCT and our field more obvious than in the ISLLC-ELCC standards. Agyris (1972) has identified the nature of rationality in some closed system strategies as comprising the following characteristics:

- economic efficiency as the ultimate criterion
- planning, setting standards and control
- task specialization
- chain of command and span of control
- use of experts, rules, rewards and sanctions (p. 20).

The master narrative (or metanarrative) which lies behind these characteristics has been described by Thompson (1967):

> The rational model of an organization results in everything being functional—-making a positive, indeed an optimum, contribution to the overall result. All resources are appropriate resources, and their allocations fits a master plan. All action is appropriate action, and its outcomes are predictable (p. 6).

The rational choice model places a premium on prediction and control. When Murphy, Yff & Shipman (2000) declared that the derivation of the ISLLC standards did not examine all of the tasks of educational leaders, but instead concentrated on the perceived "core technology" and relegated everything else to "the service of school improvement and student performance" (p. 23), they employed a familiar tactic in the reduction of uncertainty within a closed system of logic. The reduction of variables by imposing the concept of a "technical core" increases certainty and is compatible with the attainment of greater rationality between inputs and outputs (Thompson, 1967, p. 11).

The parallelism between Thompson's closed system of logic and the explanation for how the ISLLC standards were created is illuminating. Thompson (1967) notes that, "The closed-system strategy seeks certainty by incorporating only those variables positively associated with goal achievement and subjecting them to a monolithic control network" (p. 13). The parallelism for the ISLLC standards is the claim that "there is a single set of standards that applies to all leadership positions" followed by "the focus and ground of the standard should be the core of productive leadership" (Murphy, Yff & Shipman, 2000, p. 23).

A perusal of the ISSLC-ELCC standards and indictors and the repetitious use of the word "all" throughout them (Hessel & Holloway, 2002) is compatible with the type of system logic that such "technical cores" demand. They are congruent with efficiency means/ends analyses, as well as with the epistemological perspectives of behaviorism, structuralism and economic rational choice theory in which prediction and control are tightened.

For example, in describing how a vision is developed and implemented in a school to comply with the ISSLC-ELCC standards, Shipman, Queen & Peel (2007) stipulate that: (1) the principal determines the non-negotiables; (2) the principal develops an open process; and (3) the principal guides consensus building (p.13). In this perspective, the picture of humanity for both leaders and followers is tightly proscribed. In short, human agency is reduced. Albert Einstein once lamented, ". . . we have learned that rational thinking does not suffice to solve the problems of our social life" (Clark, 1971, p. 596). Concomitantly Chris Argyris (1972) once said about the de-facing of the individual in social science models, ". . . man, the human being, with feelings, needs, defenses, interpersonal relations, group dynamics is beyond their theory" (p. 24).

The common core and its regnant epistemologies are enshrined in the legalistic embrace of accreditation, licensure, and academic degrees linked to the ISLLC-ELCC standards. It isn't that these intertextual influences are wrong, rather it is that they lock out theoretical and conceptual alternatives as they become political expressions in bureaucratic agencies connected to licensure. My particular concern is the repression of the full human face of leadership.

This kind of intertextuality serves to marginalize some scholars "whose approach diverges from prevailing orthodoxy . . . [in which] all contribute to a pervasive positivism that silences critical thinking about the present socioeconomic system" (Willis, 2005, p. B11). This is one reason why concerns for social justice have not been part of the ISLLC-ELCC standards and for the most part why these standards reinforce the socio-economic status quo (see Bogotch, 2008).

Another result is the effacement of all that is considered subjective and therefore unscientific in a study of leadership. This would include the artistic, the emotional, and the role of culture in establishing the context in which leadership is manifested. Maxcy (1994) commented upon this exclusion when he wrote:

The self has been forced out of the picture as structuralists sought to explain how organizations developed in terms of the interrelations of their parts. Modernist painters performed surgery on our conventional understanding of the autonomous person, laying out the parts in disarray on the canvas. Social scientists further evacuated the task of purposeful human action when they began talking about human capital (p. 110).

Perhaps Chris Argyris (1972) summarized the social science structuralist perspective best when he observed that "the variable human seems to be minimally variable and minimally human" (p. 33).

Bourdieu (1977) has spoken of the "official language," which is ordinary language captured by a specific group and invested with authority in order to bestow upon the group a socially superior position and the power of sanctions. In this act the group establishes a line between the thinkable and the unthinkable, "thereby contributing towards the maintenance of the symbolic order from which it draws its authority" (p. 21) but simultaneously objectifying the process by which "the group teaches itself and conceals from itself its own truth, inscribing in objectivity its representation of what it is and thus binding itself by this public declaration" (p. 22).

The intertextual references within the current discursive practice in doctoral studies are mutually reinforcing. They form what Bordieu (2001) has called "epistemocratic justification for the established order" (p. 34). They work to sustain symbolic and political power through an official language with congruent discursive practices.

The official language rewards and punishes those in academe and the field (see Wiens, 2006). Professors who work within that language have access to forms of institutional support and grants that those who shun the language and dominant discursive practice are denied or forego. Those professors who pursue their own "curiosity driven research" instead of the approved topics within approved channels and within approved methods of inquiry find themselves locked out or marginalized, despite the fact that some may be "renegade geniuses, squeezing money from somewhere to pay for research that revolutionizes the state of knowledge about a key topic" (Williams, 2005, p. B24).

These points about intertextual practices are not intended to lead to their effacement, but to establish that the content of the enshrined apparatus is not fixed nor inevitable in epistemological terms. The expression of the authority to practice cannot sustain itself as to its truthfulness or efficacy because it works to discourage and suppress competing perspectives. Its greatest error is that it fails to see its own exclusions in its expositions of what should be. In other words, it is blind to its own blindness. Increased calls for "better" research or "improved rigor" are almost always calls to conduct more inquiry within the dominant discursive practices.

For example, in a review of published articles in the *Educational Administration Quarterly* 1979–2003, Murphy, Vriesenga and Storey (2007) note that the largest portion, between 38.9 and 63.6 percent, of the 221 articles published in the three time periods analyzed, were empirical studies. At the same time only 2.3 to 28.6 percent of the articles represented theoretical/conceptual analyses. The second largest category was what the reviewers called "essays" which they defined as an effort at critique, case building, or explanation (Murphy, Vriesenga & Storey, 2007, p. 615). Commenting on this trend the authors decry "the near absence of theoretical and integrative review work in the journal" (p. 627), and advocate fewer essays and more empirical work.

What is apparently not understood by Murphy, Vresenga and Storey is that empirical work is almost always undertaken within established theories and thus it is not the means by which new theories would be discovered. Feyerabend (1993) perhaps said it best when he observed, "Experience arises together with theoretical assumptions not before them, and an experience without theory is just as incomprehensible" (p. 149). Feyerabend (1995) further elaborates "Experience, taken by itself, is mute. It does not provide any means of establishing a connection with a language unless one already includes in it some elementary linguistic rules, i.e., unless one again refers to tradition" (p. 37).

Most empirical research uses an inductive approach in which certain facts or variables are tested as producing an effect. They are, inevitably, theory impregnated. So no new constructs or theories are likely to emanate from such investigations. In other words, empiricist work cannot make a subject of study that which it cannot conceive, or as Usher and Edwards (1996) observe, an emphasis which centers only on the observable "cannot conceive the unconscious in itself" (p. 73):

> This relates to science's obsession with the quest for presence. Hence the emphasis on verification which guarantees presence by removing all possibility of error—a certainty attained by the termination of uncertainty (p. 73).

Instead, new theoretical constructs are much more likely to stem from critical essays of the status quo than from empirical studies. When critics of current educational research call for more rigor, they almost always do so within the empiricist tradition (see Levin, 2006; Seashore Louis & Honig, 2007). However, improved rigor is not likely to yield new theoretical or conceptual breakthroughs within the empiricist legacy. The reason is that there is a difference between discovery and validation. Empirical work rarely leads to discovery of new concepts or theories. On the other hand, it is a necessity to validate a discovery. This distinction is one of the reasons that Paul Feyerabend (1993) observed that "successful research does not obey general standards; it relies now on one trick, now on another; the moves that advance it and the standards that define what counts as an advance are not always known to the movers" (p. 1). I think we can put aside the idea that more "rigorous" research within existing lines of inquiry and with wholly empirical methods will lead to any significant breakthroughs in practice. In this respect "more rigor" pertains to matters of verification as opposed to matters of discovery.

The Restoration of Human Agency: The Current Cosmogony of Educational Leadership as a Field of Study and Preparation

I want to turn now to the current cosmogony of educational leadership. Figure 4 is an attempt to more precisely illustrate how our ontology, ideologies and epistemologies work in harmony to create a cosmogony or a specific frame of reference for our field. Armstrong (2005) has indicated that a functional cosmogony is the intersection of reality and actual events, but that such an intersection is never objective

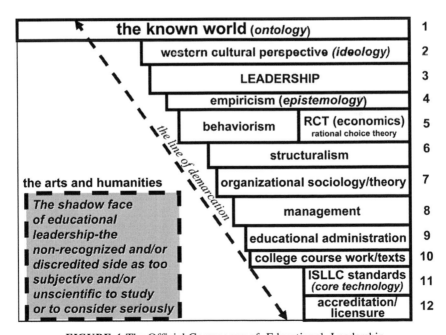

FIGURE 4 The Official Cosmogony of Educational Leadership.

in that people cannot live outside of it and often do not even understand it is not "natural."

I begin a discussion of Figure 4 by noting that no one ever sees everything in their environment. George Tice (1977) observed, ". . . you can only see what you are ready to see—what mirrors your mind at that particular time" (as cited in Sontag, p.197). Vision is never total in this sense. Reality is so overwhelming and so multi-dimensional and all at once, that much of it has to be screened out for humans to function. Peirce (1934) spoke about *synechism*, a term he used to describe the totality of reality and commented that, "Reality is a continuum which swims in indeterminancy" (p. 171).

The biggest lens that is constructed from birth is culture. Culture is so pervasive and interwoven with language, conceptualization and vision, that we rarely realize that our reality is a social construction and not "natural" at all. It is within culture that a human learns to use language, "actions, postures, gestures, tones of voice, facial expressions, the way he handles time, space, materials, and the way he works, plays, makes love, and defends himself" (Hall, 1981, p. 42).

For example the Western way of gazing at humankind, rooted in the ancient Greek *logos*, marks the Western mindscape as different—not better, but different. The Greek perspective is identified as containing a series of binaries, either-or logic demarcations, where one is "either" or "or". The term "other" refers to the "or" part of the binary. The Greek line of argument privileges the first term in the binary. That is always the main one, the dominant one. The second term is the alternative, the subordinate part of the binary.

We see the results of such binaries in our own discourse: rational/irrational; male/female; heterosexuality/homosexuality; science/non-science; white/black; quantitative/qualitative; thinking/emotion; practice/theory; truth/myth; fact/fancy; and civilized/primitive to cite a few. Greek logic is centered in a specific kind of discourse laced with binaries. It is what comprises a "decision-tree" model of decision making. It anchors our views of what makes for effective decision making and it is congruent with notions of effective management, a sub-set of leadership as shown in Figure 4.

The dominant Greek cognitive perspective permeates discussions regarding leadership. Since Greek logic is embedded in scientific discourse and the idea of the rational, it has become privileged in Western discourse. It is no small wonder that our idea of leadership and the models of it that are embedded in the social sciences and economics reflect an approach to trying to grasp the dynamics of what is part and parcel of total humanity outside this discourse. And it is hard to understand how they fail to produce only a limited understanding at the same time.

Science has become the dominant world view in Western culture. Yet science itself has many built-in problems, not the least of which is that it is as open to falsehood, superstition, prejudice, and bias as any other human endeavor. Scientists are as receptive as any other human beings to negative cultural stereotypes and prejudices because they begin their lives, not as scientists but as participants in the larger society. The common language they use is part and parcel of the general cultural discourse of the social classes in which they were born and reared (see Lewontin, 1991; Bourdieu, 1984). The interlocking perspectives of behaviorism, rational choice theory from economics, structuralism and organizational sociology/organizational theory anchor the notions of management within which educational administration as a field is thoroughly contoured (see also Young & Lopez, 2005).

While scholars in education administration often write about the quest for rationality and social science legitimacy (see Culbertson, 1988; Donmoyer, 1999), few textbook authors in our field acknowledge their own epistemological stance in presenting this quest, and rarely if ever subject it to the scrutiny of revealing its own silences and presuppositions even as they are introducing new students to academic study (see Hoy & Miskel, 1982; Haller & Strike, 1986; Owen, 1987; Hanson, 1991; Cunningham & Cordeiro, 2000). So it is not surprising that not many of our graduates really understand the gaps and lapses in what they have learned as factual matters or seriously question the expressions of certainty in the rationality of the social sciences as embodied in the ISLLC-ELCC standards.

Bourdieu (1984) has expressed this rather fundamental issue as one involving a false kind of objectivity:

> The objectification is always bound to remain partial, and therefore false, so long as it fails to include the point of view from which it speaks and so fails to construct the game as a whole (p. 12).

The derivation of the ISLLC-ELCC standards is marked singularly by the failure of the proponents to identify their epistemological presuppositions or the ahistorical nature of their claims, even as they acknowledge that they did not include the full range of the actual nature of leadership responsibilities, but instead concentrated on the "core technology" of the job, a much narrower sub-set of the school leadership role (Murphy, 2000).

It is upon this extreme miniaturization of our field (rows 11 and 12 in Figure 4) that reviews of educational administration programs are conducted and policed by NCATE. The policing function exerts enormous pressure on programs and disproportionately skews the nature of the curriculum and judgments about the efficacy of a program's offerings. It disproportionately weights the de-skilled and reified ISLLC-ELCC standards in the courses and curriculum, and embodies an extreme form of anti-intellectualism, an anti-change and anti-theoretical lens that exemplifies the scholasticism of our times.

This development has become a major barrier to the long-term health of our discipline, even as at the same time it facilitates the transfer of practitioner preparation to alternative, non-university and for-profit organizations. The future of our field lies in its ability to push the boundaries of knowledge forward instead of consolidating and reifying past practices.

What the NCATE process does is to shift the focus to the past and severely erode the need for any new knowledge and more perniciously, any new theoretical exploration as unnecessary. If all we do is to offer a vocational curriculum we can easily be replaced by those who will do it better and cheaper, a trend already visible, as shown below in Part 2.

The Restoration of Human Agency: Towards the Re-Emergence of the Arts and Humanities in Preparing School Leaders

I demur on the point that the effectiveness of school leaders will be enhanced by moving their preparation to schools of business or replacing the Ed.D. with the MBA (English, 2008a). All those recommendations would do is continue the trajectory of the last fifty years (see Callahan, 1962); or as Born (1996) observed, "the current state of leadership studies [is] overwhelmingly dominated by the paradigms of social psychology and business management" (p. 57). Proponents who advocate such measures are generally unaware of the history of our field and its intellectual and conceptual roots. We are all the children of Frederick Taylor and his legacy lives on in schools of business, education, industrial education and public administration (see Crow & Grogan, 2005; Samier, 2005). As long as we remain in intellectual thrall to a hegemonic Taylorism and its derivative, total quality management, we are not likely to learn more about leadership. For us to do that, we must restore the shadow side of the face of leadership (refer back to Figure 1) in the arts and humanities because they "are exactly about cultural constructions of leadership and power" (Born, 1996, p. 57).

Lawrence Cremin (1965) observed the same phenomena nearly a half century ago when he wrote:

> I think we need to train up a new kind of educational leader in this country if the great questions of educational purpose are to receive intelligent discussion by teachers and the lay public. This new kind of leader will obviously need fundamental preparation in the humanities of education, those studies of history, philos-

ophy, and literature that will enable him to develop a clear and compelling vision of education and of its relation to American life (pp. 117–8).

The restoration of the full face of leadership begins then at the top of Figure 4 with the recognition that leadership is a cultural construct deeply embedded in the mythos of a specific society, its central beliefs, stories and symbols (rows 1 and 2). The function of myths within any given culture is that they create, maintain and legitimate possible past, present and future actions; they originate and conceal political interests and the values supporting them; they assist in connecting cause and effect relationships when knowledge about them is incomplete; and they rationalize complexity and instability to enable decisions and actions to be made in conditions of uncertainty (Turner, 1990: pp. 3–4).

The restoration of the full face for leadership must also move beyond the established social science traditions of behaviorism, structuralism and rational choice theory as a derivative of economic game theory. It is important to note that these social science traditions have all but erased emotion as a catalyst of decision-making (see Bolton & English 2009), and likewise eroded substantive discussion of the place of values, ethics and moral conduct or what Bandura (2001) has called *agentive acts*. Agentive acts embrace the "prime features of humanness such as subjectivity, deliberative self-guidance, and reflective self-reactiveness" (p. 3).

In Bandura's (2001) social cognitive theory we see the coming together of humans acting on joint beliefs. That confluence is not "a disembodied group mind" or an "emergent entity that operates independently of the beliefs and actions of the individuals who make up a social system" (p. 14). Bandura's recasting of the perspective of individuals acting on their beliefs is a restoration of human agency and its power in human life. While a human works with a human social system, that human possesses the power to act independently within and from it.

The restoration of human agency, the idea that one individual human being is important and can bring about change in human life, in society, and in organizations such as schools, means also returning to an inclusive view of the role of culture, language, values and mythology in examining the importance of leaders in society and in schools. Paul Johnson (1996) summarized it as follows:

> Leadership is an empirical phenomenon conducive to study from a descriptive, social scientific, and value-free standpoint. . . . It is also an inherently humanistic concern whose ambiguities, contextuality, and normativity require the interpretive methods and devices of history, literature, and philosophy (among others). No account of leadership can be complete, or completely adequate, unless it makes some explicit attempt to integrate these two methodological perspectives (p. 14)

Both sides of the face of educational leadership must function for us to have any chance of achieving a breakthrough in understanding how to improve the effectiveness of leaders in their current positions and how to prepare better leaders in the future. To do that we must alter the existing cosmogony of preparation and practice. That also means dissolving the kinds of historical binaries that have dominated the intellectual landscape of our field such as objective/subjective; rational/non-rational; scientific/unscientific; logical/illogical; theory/practice; masculine/feminine that pervade our current discourse.

The Need for Competing Research Paradigms

The interlocking epistemologies and viewpoints shown in Figure 4 (rows 4–7) not only illustrate the narrowness of our current set of standards (rows 11 and 12) for preparing school administrators, but they also illustrate a mind frame about how to conduct inquiry and research into improving practice. For want of a better term, they might be called a *paradigm* after the work of the Thomas Kuhn (1962).

Paradigm has become a much over-used term, especially at the present time, but as Kuhn used it, a *paradigm* was a sort of mental heuristic employed by scientists working within a commonly understood set of assumptions. What was important about Kuhn's premise was that (1) "normal science" was characterized by the presence of a dominant paradigm, and (2) those who believed in the dominant paradigm worked to repress or relegate alternative perspectives to an "otherness" category, either one of "non-science" and hence not worthy of any serious consideration, or to something which wasn't even non-science, i.e., the absurd. So those working in a paradigm were intolerant of anything different from what they believed.

Lakatos (1999) and others characterized Kuhn's notion of *paradigm* as an abnormal situation in science. What was normal they contended was the presence of competing paradigms (or research programs as Lakatos termed them). Lakatos (1999) then proposed a way of contending with the "demarcation problem." This problem presented itself because there are no good ways to prove or disprove theories. An extended time period is needed to determine which research program (or paradigm) is indeed the correct one to follow.

Lakatos (1999) spoke of how those advocating one research program could also create ways of dealing with new facts unanticipated by their perspective without abandoning the theory itself. Only after much work would a theory which was not as fecund to explain novel facts actually be abandoned by its adherents. Lakatos (1999) proposed that this notion of competing paradigms be the one to replace Kuhn's concept of paradigm dominance.

It is my belief that Lakatos' proposition about setting up competing paradigms be employed in exploring new dimensions of educational leadership today. However, that perspective runs counter to the last fifty years in our field in which we were searching for one and then another paradigm to understand leadership and simultaneously establish and maintain academic recognition in the social sciences at the university (Culbertson, 1999).

I think that the social science perspectives we have adopted (rows 4–9 in Figure 4) have been mined out in what remains to understand about leadership. We have to broaden our search and I believe that will occur by restoring the side of the face of leadership anchored in the arts and humanities for that is where discovery lies in the future. However, instead of encouraging alternative views of leadership and with it alternative perspectives and methods of inquiry, the government and the private foundations have sunk millions into verification procedures. Verification pertains to what already exists and what we already know. I don't see any dramatic new breakthroughs as a result of their investments, and I think the chances are pretty good there won't be any until there is a shift in the focus of inquiry to restore opportunities for discovery as opposed to pursuing forms of verification.

If the history of scientific breakthroughs in other fields provides a clue to our own dilemma it is that such occurrences are rarely planned and do not occur along predicted lines within established theories. They are "out of paradigm" and no amount of planned research within prevailing mind frames would have produced them (see LeFanu, 1999). This is all the more reason to prefer a state in practice and research that encourages very radical perspectives to be tested and to insist on pursuing multiple research programs instead of trying to find the "one best one" to fund. I appreciate the words of Niels Bohr, the Danish Nobel Prize winner, who said that really promising theories had to be "really crazy" and violate common sense to hold much promise for a new and fundamental breakthrough (Gratzer, 2002, p. 42).

A Synoptic Manifesto for Change in Educational Administration/Leadership

What is set forth here are some proposals for change in not only the way we have done business in the past, but more importantly how we have thought about what we were doing in the past. They are organized around the question, "What does it mean to restore human agency in preparation, practice, theory development and research?" Taken together they constitute a synoptic manifesto for change in educational administration.

Such a manifesto cannot be painted on a blank canvas, for there is much already present in our context that represents decisions and roads taken that are contrary to where I believe the field has to go. They will be difficult to reverse, especially as the many agencies and associations represented in Figure 2 within the current educational apparatus have a vested interest in maintaining the status quo in which their power is vested. For that reason I don't believe true change will come from the outside. External forces, although in some instances well financed, as in the case of the Broad Foundation and the Thomas B. Fordham Institute's (2003) *Better Leaders for America's Schools: A Manifesto,* are essentially political broadsides not aimed at impacting theory or practice, but at altering the legislative and policy landscape (see DeMarrais 2006; O'Conner, 2007).

And I see little change occurring in a well-financed study and subsequent report by Arthur Levine (2005). Despite the fact that Levine, as an education dean, was labeled an insider by some, the educational leadership community never considered him so. In addition, his research methods in conducting the study violated the responsibility to make public data used in support of evidential claims.

Thus, I see significant change as having to come from the inside. It has to emerge as the result of the leadership within the educational apparatus being persuaded that the current course is unwise and will not result in the publicly proclaimed objectives they all want to accomplish. So this manifesto is aimed squarely at those leaders, their practitioner and professor colleagues, and professional society members.

The restoration of human agency is not an "either-or" proposal. The abandonment of traditional social science methods is not advocated. These methods are essential for validating new discoveries, but they are not likely to yield such discoveries. Verification has to be logical. But on the other hand, *discovery* is fanciful. This led Feyerabend (1993) to say, "Without chaos no knowledge. Without a frequent dismissal of reason, no progress" (p. 158). Furthermore, since educational leadership is in the main a moral enterprise centered on social, ethical and cultural values, the restoration of human agency signals a return to the arts and humanities as part of our expanded discourse. Without such an expansion I see the essential social justice agenda still relegated to the fringes of our field, because there is no science of values in social science world views.

As an example of a far-reaching leadership perspective, Temes (1996) discusses Martin Luther King's "Letter from a Birmingham Jail," issued in 1963. Temes indicates that the letter, a manifesto in its own right, was an exercise in ideational leadership (p. 74):

> By this I mean that King did not merely refer to the ideas that drove him, but he explained them in careful detail. His mode of leadership was almost entirely philosophical, and almost entirely impersonal—he made no claims for himself, or for any other man or woman, but demanded attention to ideas (p. 74).

King's version of human agency in the civil rights struggle was centered by ideas. This led Temes (1996) to define leadership as, "...the action of ideas to make change through the agency of individuals" (p. 74). And the ideas that grounded King's leadership were that good and evil were always present and in constant conflict with one another; that a peace which cloaks or constrains this struggle is deleterious; and that institutional authority is not enough to determine the difference between good and evil (Temes, 1996, p. 74).

It would be hard to find a more powerful example of the importance of human agency than Martin Luther King in America. Without grasping his commitment to values one could not adequately understand his power and lasting influence as a leader. The restoration of human agency in the study of leadership is essential to fully appreciate how individual leaders can and have made a difference, but as Temes (1996) warns, King's philosophical centered leadership "cuts directly against the technique-centered approach to teaching leadership" (p. 75). That approach dominates our college and university curricula at the masters' level and also very heavily at the doctoral level in educational administration today (see Figure 3).

A Consideration of the False Premises Which Serve to Negate the Need for a Restored Perspective of Human Agency in Educational Leadership

I want to review the false premises I believe stand in the way of restoring human agency in the preparation of educational leaders. While some represent positions taken by individuals, many are simply world views or perspectives that inhibit reconceptualizing how a more human face in our preparation courses would improve practice and open the doors to a more adequate understanding of what leaders really do (see Duke, 1989; Gardner, 1991; Rost, 1991; Starratt, 1993; Ackerman and Maslin-Ostrowski, 2002; Blasé & Blasé, 2003; Bottery, 2004; Crow & Grogan, 2005; Samier, 2005; English, 2008, 2008b; Lumby & English, 2009; Samier & Atkins, 2009).

False Premise #1. Educational Leadership Practices Will Be Significantly Improved by Codifying, Homogenizing and Standardizing Them

True breakthroughs in the study of improved educational leadership in the schools are unlikely to occur by codifying current practices, extending internships, removing preparation from the university setting, creating local academies run by practitioners or the business community, linking them to licensure, or testing them via state examinations. What these approaches will do is create a homogeneity of practice. Homogeneity cannot be equated to any form of excellence, for as Charles Sanders Pierce (1955) so eloquently explained, "Direct experience is neither certain nor uncertain, because it affirms nothing—it just is" (p. 67).The codification of existing notions of practice offers no insurance that they are not filled with errors and falsehoods similar to those which have plagued the medical profession and other applied disciplines over hundreds of years.

The so-called "wisdom of field" (Murphy, 2000) has augured prominently in the construction of the ISLLC-ELCC standards. Local leadership academies centered on the standards and other popular notions of management are fraught with the possibilities of errors, and there is little to do about extending them for more practitioners without some means of testing their efficacy. Because the ISLLC-ELCC standards are thoroughly embedded in current practices, they support the status quo and function as a barrier to any significant theoretical alternatives regarding leadership.

False Premise #2. The Current Cosmogony of Educational Leadership is Adequate to Solve All the Challenges Facing Schools Today

The proponents of the ISLLC-ELCC standards admit to no shortcomings. There are no statements in the texts of the proponents that if all of the standards were faithfully implemented every problem in the schools today would not be resolved. The unwritten assumption therefore has to be that all major problems within the schools will be successfully resolved if only the standards are implemented with fidelity.

Figure 4 illustrates how the concept of leadership has been miniaturized by an interlocking epistemocratic worldview (a cosmogony) of empiricism, behaviorism, rational choice theory, structuralism and organizational sociology (theory) which is congruent with traditional management theory centered on prediction, control and efficiency. This epistemocratic worldview is reinforced by extant textbooks which espouse the same perspective, even as they acknowledge alternatives but in purely subordinate (and inferior) terms (see Willower, 1994).

The inability of those working within the social science framework to recognize their own presuppositions and prejudices is one of the historic flashpoints in the profession's denial, reluctance and continued resistance in dealing with prevalent biases against women, persons of color, and gays and lesbians in the ranks of practitioners and professors (see Blount 1998, 2005; Lopez, 2003; Lumby & Coleman, 2007; Tillman, 2002, 2003). This cultural blind spot still exists within the profession and fuels the attention of many professors and committed practitioners to social justice issues both within and outside of educational administration (see Shoho, Merchant & Lugg, 2005; Marshall & Oliva, 2006).

The traditional social science cosmogony eliminates such human issues as race, sexuality and gender as not relevant to its perspective or to a sanitized version of management in which motivation, intention, values and ethics are not very important to rational decision making. Attention to these matters is seen as too "subjective" to be taken into account in our field, and when applied internationally the presence of this "scientific rationalism" based on economically derived mathematical models "is both the expression and the justification of a Western arrogance which leads people to act as if they had the monopoly on reason" (Bourdieu, 1998, p.19).

False Premise #3: Alternative Streams to Educational Leadership Are Necessary to Improve Leadership of the Schools

The current political discourse regarding educational leadership is that few current officials are sufficiently committed enough to engage in the kind of bold moves that are required to confront the complex problems of the mass educational system. To pursue innovative solutions one must recruit educational leaders from the ranks outside education, from business, the financial world and the military (See Finn, 1991; Hess, 2004; Broad Foundation and Thomas B. Fordham Institute, 2003).

Despite the fact that there are enough individuals with administrative licenses to fill vacant positions in leadership, the argument to circumvent the traditional supply streams which have been colleges and universities, is that those in line for jobs are not "really" qualified (they are certified however). Therefore, the training pipeline is faulty (see Broad Foundation and Thomas B. Fordham Institute, 2003). At the same time, the claim is advanced that the standards upon which licensure are based are unnecessary and should be erased. This will permit more qualified and creative administrators to lead the schools. To support this claim the critics have to argue that leadership is largely a genetic capacity and does not require university preparation. This eliminates the licensure prerequisite. Secondly they have to de-skill job complexity so that anyone can do it. This tactic then prepares the way for declaring that there are many, many qualified people "out there," who if the barriers were simply removed, could be "spotted, courted, recruited, and developed" (Broad Foundation & Thomas B. Fordham Institute, 2003, p. 15) to run the schools.

I have criticized this neo-liberal attack as one which is largely, if not exclusively politically motivated (English, 2004b; Giroux, 2004). First, it is a move to remove licensure and the dominant (and liberal) schools of education as production centers for school administrators. I have also advanced the claim that it is the reinsertion of gender discrimination. The basis for my claim is that educational administration, of all fields in the university, has more females in graduate classes than most others. More women are in top level administrative positions (central office roles and superintendencies) in education than in business or the military. Data provided by the National Opinion Research Center for 2002 and published in *The Chronicle of Higher Education* show that of eight fields, education awarded more doctorates to women (66%) than any other. Business awarded only 38%.

Supporting my claim that by opening up educational leadership positions to non-educators represents a move to re-masculinize our field, data supplied by Eisinger and Hula (2008) show that of the twenty-five non-educators selected to run some of the nation's largest public school systems, not one female is listed. The occupations from which these "gunslinger superintendents" were drawn were the military, politics, banking, business and law. All of these fields have much lower rates of promoting women to positions of leadership than education.

Eisinger and Hula (2008) comment about this trend as follows:

> ... the first things that nontraditional school administrators tend to do is to impose order on the chaotic bureaucratic operations of the school district. They are not educational innovators. ... They seek to bring order by streamlining, consolidating, and rationalizing, all in the effort to reduce inefficiencies and duplication and to increase accountability (p. 121).

The free market ideology once popular on Wall Street and with the neo-conservatives has fallen into some disrepute under the strictures of global recession. The shock to the free market pundits has been, as Bremmer (2009) has noted, "New York City used to be the world's financial capital. It no longer is even the financial capital of the United States . . ." (p. 49). However, leading up to the financial global crash, there has been a steady onslaught of for-profit ventures into education promoted by eight years of Republican political hegemony, from the Edison schools (Saltman, 2005) to corporations comprising the Business Round Table. The tentacles of the BRT, principally through the Institute for Educational Leadership (or the IEL) extend throughout the nation and provide linkages to our national practitioner associations such as the AASA, NAESP, NASSP, Council for Great City Schools, CCSSO and these to foundations and conservative think tanks (Emery & Ohanian, 2004, pp. 233–236).

Keeping the public in the public schools is a major task which lies ahead. The advent of the privately owned EMOs (educational management organizations) has increased substantively and as Anderson and Pini (2005) demonstrate, despite the democratic rhetoric, EMOs are principally interested in the profits they can accrue and not in innovation or even in increasing efficiency and cost-effectiveness (p. 230).

The movement towards charter schools and other alternative approaches has little to do with understanding leadership better. They simply go around the problem without stepping in the puddle. To date no bold advances in practice have emanated from them (see Carnoy, Jacobsen, Mishel & Rothstein, 2005). The notion that the free market is the best approach to promote change has been shown to be an illusion with the crash of the fiduciary giants, the collapse of the car companies, and the debacle of the housing market. The idea that "greed is good" (Caplan, 2007, p. 193) has left us in a moral vacuum and forms powerful evidence that the managerial paradigm of rational choice theory, behaviorism and structuralism which has dominated business, public administration and educational administration is culturally clueless and morally bankrupt.

Conversations with colleagues across the country have convinced me that we do a pretty poor job of awakening our graduate students to the privatizing movement underway in our educational systems. Our students are unaware of not only those efforts, but do not recognize the prevalent vocabulary in which this movement wraps its agenda in, something which Emery and Ohanian (2004) have called "ed-bizspeak" with such terms as "schools as data-driven institutions, data-driven reform, total data control, data-driven decision-making" (p. 13). Emery and Ohanian (2004) warned about the use of data without a social conscience and reminded us that "there's a close relationship between the Auschwitz tattoo and IBM data sorters: IBM supplied the data solution to the Third Reich" (p. 13).

I turn now to suggesting some steps that might be considered to restore human agency in leadership preparation and practice.

Steps to Restore Human Agency in Theory, Research and Practice OR Good Leadership is a Total Package

The full human face of the educational leader has long been erased in the study of educational administration (see Born, 1996; Gunter & Ribbins, 2002; Crow & Grogan, 2005; Ribbins, 2006; Milley, 2006). This development has been paralleled in business and public administration. (see Samier, 2005; Khurana, 2007). Even in medical training the human face of the doctor has been eclipsed by what is fast becoming known as "evidence-based medicine." Jerome Groopman (2007) describes the concept and its approach:

> . . . today's rigid reliance on evidence-based medicine risks having the doctor choose care passively, solely by the numbers. Statistics cannot substitute for the human being before you; statistics embody averages, not individuals. . . . I concluded that the next generation of doctors was being conditioned to function like a well-programmed computer that operates within a strict binary framework (p. 6).

Groopman (2007) indicates that how doctors are being trained to function in a rational, linear way in some medical schools, and then assigning probabilities following Bayesian analysis based on the construction of algorithms, and is at odds with how doctors actually practice medicine because "good doctoring is a total package" (p. 19).

Borrowing that idea, I propose that "good leadership is a total package." That is, the full humanity of the leader has to be developed within an approach that not only rests on knowledge but also understanding. Perhaps the most eloquent differentiation between these two ideas was penned by Carl Jung (1958) in his book *The Undiscovered Self:*

> Scientific education is based in the main on statistical truths and abstract knowledge and therefore imparts an unrealistic, rational picture of the world in which the individual, as a merely marginal phenomenon, plays no role. The individual, however, as an irrational datum, is the true and authentic carrier of reality, the concrete man as opposed to the unreal or normal man to whom the scientific statements refer (p. 21).

What Jung notes is that science is about knowledge while the humanities are about understanding, and for that to occur one must ". . . approach the task of understanding with a free and open mind" (p. 18). Jung is not anti-scientific. He does not advocate an abandonment of science, but rather to acquire both knowledge and understanding. In this way good leadership and preparation should be "a total package." This notion is a useful hinge upon which to propose a restoration of human agency in educational leadership theory, research and practice. A restoration is what is proposed in this book where the full human face was expected and necessary in providing leadership, and where at one time leading superintendents considered themselves "scholars and gentlemen" and not business persons (Callahan, 1962, p. 180).

The penetration of ideas regarding the preparation of school leaders from business and industry encapsulated in the ideas of efficiency (cost-cutting or cost-reduction as a result of better methods) arose in the 1840s as part of the common school movement (Berman, 1983 as cited in Campbell, Fleming, Newell & Bennion, 1987, p. 34). However, the doctrine of efficiency was given a huge push by the work of Frederick Taylor (1911) and the publication of his *Principles of Scientific Management.* Although there was little about Taylor's "principles" that were scientific (see Kanigel, 1997), they had a huge impact on the public sector, education being one of the public services whose rising costs were visible to most taxpayers.

The gist of scientific management was about its control of the work. In fact, the work was no longer defined by the worker, but by efficiency experts and then handed to the worker to perform it, thus giving rise to the practice of job de-skilling. This stratagem thoroughly penetrated educational administration and remains today in business, industry and education in many guises, not the least of which is the practice of strategic planning.

Jelinek (1979) has pointed out that Taylor's work study methods which originated on the shop floor at the Midvale Steel Works in the early 1880s, are now replicated at the top of the organizational hierarchy with strategic planning based on the same separation of work from the worker, or in this case, the tasks of management from the manager. We see the same stratagem used in the creation and implementation of the ISLLC-ELCC standards today (for an example see Owing & Kaplan, 2003). The approach is basic Taylorism in spirit and application (English, 2003).

Perhaps the most pernicious part of scientific management was the manipulation and control of the worker by designing the work based on methods rooted in efficiency which now bear the sobriquet "best practices," which is another term for "the one best method" but with the same goal in mind. And despite claims that such "best practices" are research based, just as in Taylor's day, the designation of the one best method is almost wholly a cherished "rule of thumb" (Kanigel, 1997, p. 320).

What disappeared in a montage of the educational leader prior to Taylorism was the idea that a leader was an intellectual, one steeped in human thought over a wide range of issues and human experiences in the humanities, especially intellectual currents that pertained to values, ethics and morality. That was all to be replaced with efficiency engineering.

Gone were the days when William Torrey Harris (1835–1909), Superintendent of the St. Louis Public Schools (1868–1880) and later the fourth U.S. Commissioner of Education (1889–1906), was known as one of the leading philosophers of education along with John Dewey, translated Hegel into English, founded and edited a journal of speculative philosophy, and was known to have interrupted his evening meal when a stranger knocked at his door and wanted to talk philosophy, or a person met him on a crowded streetcar and as a straphanger initiated a philosophical conversation (Leidecker, 1946, p. 571).

And this educational leader was an uncompromising innovator for the American common school that included a curriculum that enabled public school students to understand the culture of the larger society, the first to install a permanent kindergarten program, and advocated the teaching of the curriculum in the native language of the students instead of in English. Such a school leader today would be an anachronism in America. School leaders steeped in the tenets of total quality management which thoroughly permeate the ISLLC-ELLC standards and the mythology of "managerial perfectionism" (see Pattison, 1997) are now the norm. But the portrait of William Torrey Harris, who not without his faults at the time, serve as stark reminders of what we have traded away in concepts of educational leadership as well as what we need to regain.

The movement away from the full human face of leadership was accelerated with the "theory movement" in educational administration. This movement began in 1957 when 50 professors from 20 leading universities gathered at the University of Chicago to begin a conversation about "administrative theory in education" (Culbertson, 1995, p. 34). Essentially this group's seminar marked the beginnings of the founding of UCEA, which officially began in 1959 (Fusarelli, 2006, p. 1044).

According to Culbertson (1995) the seminar agreed to advance the ideas that the notions of the Vienna Circle and logical positivism should be adopted in our field; that imagination must be subordinated to observation; methods in the natural sciences should be applied to social and human phenomena; the idea of the "hypothetico-deductive system" was adopted to join mathematics with "real world" experience; a true science was not interested in "what should be" but rather "what is"; and that in pursuing these goals the field of educational administration should be inclusive and adopt ideas from other fields of administration. The key book at the time was Herbert Simon's (1947) text *Administrative Behavior* in public administration and the accompanying idea of explaining human behavior and decision making around the concept of "economic man". I have described this development as a "fateful turn" in our field (English, 2002). It is a turn from which we are still trying to extricate ourselves.

What the theory movement did was (refer to Figure 4) erase the face of the full, purposive and moral educational leader, because moral behavior is situated in "the ought to be world" rather than the one which exists. But science does not deal with the "ought to be" at least not the science embraced in 1957 and encapsulated in hypothetico-deductive models. The theory movement also cemented the field's epistemology firmly in behaviorism, structuralism and organizational sociology/theory (rows 4–7). Our research focus remains primarily centered in these rows as well. Educational administration quickly became management and connected to licensure and relevant course work.

Early intellectual work by such professors as Jacob Getzels (1958) proposed that educational administration was concerned first structurally within a hierarchy of superior-subordinate relationships and functionally within the hierarchy the locus for allocating and integrating roles to attain the goals of the social system (p. 151) Getzels defined a social system as "involving two classes of phenomena which are at once conceptually independent and phenomenally interactive" (p. 152). The first was concerned with institutional roles connected to the goals of the system, which he named *nomothetic,* and the second group of roles, the individual's personality and need-dispositions, were named *idiographic.* Getzels' motivation in sketching out this canvas was that "to understand the nature of observed behavior—and to be able to predict and control it—we must understand the nature and relationship of these elements" (p. 152).

The development of organizational theory as a more or less permanent feature in preparation programs for educational leaders was the outcome of an attempt to forge a science of educational leadership by creating a science of organization and erasing the so-called "irrational elements" of humans such as emotion, intuition, whimsy, and fear as not relevant, because they were unscientific in an empirical-behavioral-sociological worldview (see Hills, 1969).

The ascendance of Simon's "economic man" as the supreme embodiment of rationality remains embedded in the ISLLC-ELCC standards today. The full embrace of rows 4–12 in Figure 4 within a social science framework was perceived also to elevate educational administration and schools of education on university campuses and to edge the field away from the arts and humanities. The search for greater on-campus prestige and enhanced legitimacy in the academy has been a distinct trend in the overall history of schools of education (Shen, 1999). The downside has been a blindspot for issues such as politics, culture, and the role of K–12 schooling in the larger society as perpetuating socio-economic distance between classes and thus reproducing them (see Bowles & Gintis, 1976; Bourdieu-Passeron, 2000).

It is instructive to review one of the earliest analyses of the troubles of urban school superintendents by Larry Cuban (1976), which involved their responses to larger socio-economic issues in their cities, in this case, San Francisco, Chicago and Washington, D.C. As the crises escalated, the model of leadership each unsuccessfully employed did in fact fit perfectly into the prescriptions of the theory movement and how that movement portrayed the essentials of leadership. Each of the superintendents adopted a rational model of response in which "the scenario accepts organizational decision-making as flowing from the powerful inner drive of the system, but assumes that the process is manageable and subject to sensitive calibration by efficient administrators" (p. 109).

The heuristic at work in the minds of Cuban's superintendents was one we teach in most organizational theory classes, namely, that "[their] responses to demands were system solutions for which each large organization had already developed programmed responses" (p. 108). The tenets of human agency, the need for a full range of human emotion to be present in their decision-making, were viewed as irrational and not relevant. That is the field we still teach today.

What I hope I have illustrated here is that it is necessary to restore the full face of the human in educational leadership. The idea that an individual human being as a leader can make an enormous difference must be re-established in our preparation programs, our theories and our research. We are not likely to arrive at any substantive understanding of leadership until that happens. But to do that we must recognize that our epistemocratic framework is too narrow and our field is too insular. Our theory, research and practice suffer as a consequence.

Let me now roughly sketch out the steps I believe we must take to accomplish the proposed restoration of human agency. Given the limited time and space I have, they should be considered only propaedeutic. I have given no thought to how difficult some of these recommendations will be or to which ones may be "feasible" or not. It seems to me that these are the steps we should undertake. I am reminded of the remark by Albert Einstein, "I have little patience with scientists who take a board of wood, look for its thinnest part, and drill a great number of holes where drilling is easy" (Frank, 1949). I am aware that some of the recommendations will not be easily implemented.

1. Revise our curricula and courses to include studies in the humanities and arts. Reach out to colleagues in those fields for assistance. Add significant readings sometimes external to the field to be able to think outside the prevailing epistemocratic (behavioral/social science, rational technical) perspective. Avoid "kitsch" management texts as easy bromides to complex problems.

If we are serious about restoring human agency to issues of leadership involving moral, ethical and value based decisions that leaders confront in schools, then we need to revamp the courses and curricula to include more than the social sciences and an empiricist, behavioral, economic (RCT), structural, organizational sociology epistemocratic perspective (rows 4–10 in Figure 4). I aver that we have done a disservice to our students by submerging human agency within the dominant social science system perspective (rows 4–12 in Figure 4). By so doing we almost always ensure that our students will be confined to issues of management (row 8 in Figure 4) instead of ascending to leadership (row 3 in Figure 4).

My view after having taught all the courses in educational administration except school law in six different universities in as many states, is that the value of organizational theory as a single class is highly overrated and should be dropped and re-situated in a course which provides sociological theory as one of many views about understanding leadership, because as Spencer Maxcy (2006) has indicated "leading does not occur in a vacuum, but rather is rooted in our deepest beliefs about humankind, nature, and the real world around us," (p. 65), we also need to require our students to read outside our field and to read deeply.

I am not referring to popular management books that Samier (2005) has labeled "kitsch," which include texts produced by Stephen Covey, Ken Blanchard, Spencer Johnson, Jim Collins, Malcolm Gladwell, John Maxwell and many others. I have compiled a list of these works which offer simple bromides to complex issues replete with happy endings (see English, 2008b, pp. 160–6). Instead, for matters of values, morality and ethics it would be hard to beat Shakespeare (see Bloom, 1998) and other forms of life writing, from Plutarch (Lamberton, 2001) to Suetonius' Twelve Caesars (Graves, 1979; Whittemore, 1988) that have been historically pivotal in the education of leaders over time, from Gandhi to Churchill (English, 1995; English & Steffy, 1997; English 2006b). I am also proposing such texts as Joseph Campbell's (1973) *The Hero with a Thousand Faces* to understand the universal leadership journey in mythology; Kate Rousmaniere's (2005) *Margaret Haley: Citizen teacher: The life and leadership of Margaret Haley* as a portrait of a down to earth social justice educator, and Robert Caro's (2002) *The Years of Lyndon Johnson: Master of the Senate* for a superb mix of human interiority and contextual interactions. Human agency is about the inner human, not simply the one who "behaves" but the one who thinks, feels, and dreams before he/she *acts.*

In proffering these suggestions I am aware of the skepticism and anti-intellectualism that has permeated our classrooms from graduate students who want to study only practical information relevant to running schools. Many see little point in learning about anything that is not of immediate application in the microcosm. Instead of being practical they are impractical. Educational administration is not fundamentally about how to schedule classes or balance the budget. We are responsible for the development of human beings. As Kant noted, humans ought never be the means to ends, since they are the ends.

Our profession is a value-laden, culturally constructed and sanctioned center of life in a society where the most important issues are about the matters and meanings of life itself. This is not to suggest that it isn't important to know how to schedule properly. Rather it is to argue that the more important matter is to know what students are being scheduled to learn and become. For that we need more than managers. We need leaders who understand human agency. Without such knowledge they may be preparing students as little more than efficient bureaucratic factotums.

A major issue is that the dominant cosmogony in our field is blind to matters of culture and the artistic dimensions of administrative practice in the schools (see Bates, 2006). To overcome this sightlessness we have to seek partnerships with faculty in the arts and humanities to jointly teach some of our courses.

It is interesting to note that the shift in U.S. military strategy in Afghanistan is not to employ mightier weapons, but to engage in what is now being billed as a "culturally sensitive campaign" to win the hearts and minds of the people, a tactic which has led to some success in Iraq (Spiegel, 2009).

The military has had to learn the lessons of restoring human agency to considerations of leadership by taking into account more than rational-technical decisions which rest on mathematical probabilities derived from game theory for battlefield success. This is especially true with counterinsurgencies. The newly approved General for Afghanistan, Stanley McChrystal has not only had conventional military training, but also "yearlong stints at Harvard University and the Council for Foreign Relations that he says helped expand his world view" (Spiegel, 2009, p. A6.). We need similar expansions for educational leaders in our schools.

We must step outside our familiar theoretical and conceptual boundaries and take a proactive stance on embracing human agency in our views of school administration. We must challenge the dominant western cultural view in what we teach about leadership (see Bolton & English, 2009; Lumby & English, 2009).

2. Avoid NCATE accreditation if possible as reductionism personified. Do not equate the ISLLC-ELCC standards with any measure of excellence nor even a benchmark to determine the adequacy of a preparation program since such "standards" miniaturize the problems of practice at the outset.

Make every attempt to avoid accreditation practices that impose the ISLLC-ELCC standards as the sole criterion for making determinations of the efficacy of a preparation program. Do not confuse the ISLLC-ELCC standards with benchmarks of excellence. They represent a devolution of our field to the lowest common denominator within a cosmogony that already excludes the full face of human leadership. These standards are anti-theoretical, anti-democratic and grounded in practices that preserve the status quo and miniaturize leadership thought and practice.

State departments and education boards that believe NCATE accreditation provides a benchmark of quality are mistaken and misled. If the NCATE standards did not miniaturize the field, de-skill the role of leaders leaving them less than fully prepared to face the unique contextual challenges of real schools in the real world, and if they did not exert a stultifying impact on university preparation programs, which are devoted to improving future (as opposed to current) practices via research, then the high costs of securing accreditation might be worth it. But the fact is that some of the most outstanding schools of education in the nation are not NCATE accredited (see the annual list from *U.S. News and World Report* for specifics), and neither are the new online degree programs, which are expanding across the nation. The lack of NCATE accreditation does not discourage graduate students from applying to outstanding schools of education, nor dissuade educators from securing online degrees. So where is the quality assurance NCATE ostensibly provides the profession and/or the public?

Conceptually I am not opposed to accreditation. I am opposed to a set of standards around which accreditation takes place. These have become a barrier to fully preparing educational leaders because of how the standards were formulated, the presuppositions that inform them, and the results of their application on the actual practice of leadership in the schools.

The escalating costs of accreditation, the endless demand for paper work and the "dumbing down" of the curriculum to promote "accountability" that can be readily quantified, have done and will continue to do, a major disservice to the quality of leadership preparation, especially in research-intensive university programs where faculty are supposed to be advancing knowledge to improve practice. The extreme rational-technical NCATE process is a toxic metanarrative, and an example of Weber's (1968) "iron cage," which is devoid of human agency.

3. Differentiate between discovery and verification in pursuing research. Promote and establish competing research programs/paradigms rather than working with the current epistemocratic perspective and defining "rigor" as a measure of fidelity to its presuppositions and methodologies.

In conducting inquiry in our field we often fail to differentiate between research methods that are centered on verification, and those methods and/or activities involved with true discovery. Beveridge (1950) put it this way:

> Although we cannot deliberately evoke that will-o'-the wisp, chance, we can be on the alert for it, prepare ourselves to recognize it and profit by it when it comes. . . . In research, an attitude of mind is required for discovery which is different from that required for proof, for discovery and proof are distinct processes (p. 44).

Both critics and friends of research in educational administration advocate more rigor (Levin, 2006; Levine, 2005; Seashore Louis & Honig, 2007). However, "rigor" in strategies of verification is different than in strategies of discovery. For true discovery to result, a broader range of options requires a different notion of rigor. This will be addressed below in terms of dissertation work.

The theoretical context for conducting research in educational administration has and will continue to be rows 2–9 in Figure 4. As such it doesn't matter whether that research is quantitative, qualitative or mixed-methods as long as the same epistemocratic explanation remains in place. We not only need more attention to producing traditional research (see Part 2) within the cosmogony represented in rows 2–9 (for verification), but we need more alternative, competing epistemologies and research programs (for discovery) that promise more understanding of leadership as it is practiced in the schools, something which I have referred to as "cognitive aesthetics" (English 2008, pp. 43–66).

I believe we should adopt the concept of competing research programs as advanced by Imre Lakatos (1999) and drop the idea that "normal science" consists of research program monopoly as advanced by Thomas Kuhn (1962). Concomitantly our professional associations, notably NCPEA and UCEA, need to mount a program that attempts to convince funding agencies (public and private) that no new significant breakthroughs in practice are likely to be produced until we enjoy a broader and bolder (and riskier from the agency's perspective) approach to defining and funding educational research.

The motivation for me to argue for more alternatives in research is not advocated as a cost reduction strategy, but rather as a move to increase the likelihood that breakthroughs in practice will be stimulated from multiple perspectives now lying outside the epistemocratic perspective embodied in current methodologies. As the history of breakthroughs in other applied disciplines and fields demonstrates, chance is a significant factor in the discovery process (see Beveridge, 1950; LeFanu, 1999).

Finally, in some way we need to educate those of our colleagues working on IRB (Institutional Review Boards) panels about the difference between research concerning verification and that aimed at discovery. The precision desired in IRB applications, especially regarding the questions to be used in interviews based on the larger research study, could only be answered truthfully if one already knew the responses and was only interested in verifying them. For real discovery to be a goal of research, the IRB process is antithetical to inquiry, creativity, and the flexibility needed to conduct genuine inquiry. That is, one is forced to completely fabricate a phony precision in order to obtain permission to proceed at all. This is especially the case when the researcher really doesn't know what the right questions are.

Given this set of lamentable circumstances, it is no wonder why we really don't *discover* anything in some of the research we undertake. All we do is to continue to plow the same old theoretical furrows again and again because those are the only ones for which we know the right answers. To have a chance of discovery we have to lie. I'm sure this was not the reason the IRB was established, but it is the way it works today. It is an example of the "liar's paradox" (sometimes called Epimenides paradox, see Haack, 1978, p. 136) in contemporary times, i.e., in order to have a chance of discovering the truth, one has to lie about searching for it.

4. Restore a better balance between matters of theory and practice, especially in recruiting higher education faculty and examining program curricular choices and perspectives. Locate practice in fields of practice instead of practicing practice.

There was a time in the recruitment of higher education faculty that only social science scholars were desired, especially among the more prestigious universities. Individuals who actually had been practitioners were devalued. That was a consequence of the theory movement at work in its most virulent form. Gradually, the pendulum has swung back so that higher education faculties have began to reflect more practitioner experience.

However, the pendulum has swung too far back in my opinion, especially in the dominance of the big foundations and how they are approaching improving educational practice. There is too much emphasis on past experience and timeworn concepts and methods. Many calls for proposals use the rhetoric of desiring bold changes, but the criteria used to determine what is bold, as well as the consultants used in assessing them, strongly suggest it will be the "same old, same old". So we have millions spent for verification and very little for discovery.

Personnel at foundations and government funding agencies do not appear to grasp that while true discoveries may be encountered in practice, there is no understanding of their meaning until the theories catch up. But more than likely, new theories, especially if they are not inductively derived, may be the lynchpin to define and implement a new set of bolder practices. Lakatos (1999) has spoken of the problem of inductively derived theories which violate the logic of having to use the same set of facts twice, once to derive a theory and then again to validate it. This practice produces high correlations but little predictability. It is a problem throughout the social sciences and dooms us to working predominately with strategies of verification in our research approaches.

Several times each year I receive a letter from a retired superintendent who has moved to North Carolina and wants to become a faculty member. Somewhere in their letters they say something to the effect that after having been a successful practitioner for many years, they wish to come to the university and teach their "wisdom" to educators seeking to become administrators. I search for anything in their resumes that would indicate they have any understanding of what they were practicing which made them successful. Too many practitioners cannot locate their experience on a field of practice, that is, they have no idea where their practice is on any continuum of development. In sum, they were just practicing, with little apparent consciousness of practice. If they said they were successful because student test scores went up, then at least I'd know that their practice was located on a behavioristic, rational-technical field. Instructors from this mold do our discipline a disservice, and they leave their graduate students ignorant of the means to engage in viable critical reflection.

To understand the meaning of practice, an administrator has to be able to locate his or her practice in a larger context of the definitions and meanings of their work. That process requires knowledge and understanding of what differences there are and might be in how practice is defined and ultimately improved. It means they have to know the history of administrative practice and the currents, ideas, concepts and theories in which they inevitably swim. Without this knowledge we simply have a vocational curriculum learned by rote, and we have a trade craft and not a profession. That is where the current ISLLC-ELCC standards are taking us, reinforced by NCATE accreditation and state department reviews based on those standards. Our discipline can easily be relocated to the community college if that's all we do.

5. Re-position the schools as levers to promote a more just and fair society by altering the means of the reproduction of inequalities and inequities.

The dominant epistemocratic perspective which has defined our preparation and practice in schools for the last century, despite its rhetoric to the contrary, has positioned the K–12 school system to reproduce the social injustices and inequities of the larger society. Schools are not neutral places. They embody somebody's values and perspectives. Knowledge is not neutral. And "knowledge is power," because it works to benefit some and not others.

Schools are socially contested places. They are the arenas where the battle for whose values are to dominate society is fought and determined. While the outcomes are often not precise, especially in a democratic society, they are definitive, if only for a time. For the most part, schools are controlled by the social elites, the ones with sociopolitical power and it's that sector which defines, controls, and regulates what schools do.

School administrators "fit in" to this structure and they have a responsibility to protect it, defend it, and I would argue, *change it* so that the injustices, prejudices, inequities, and discrimination that have left us with the baggage of racism, sexism, homophobia and economic disadvantage are ultimately removed from the larger body politic. This perspective envisions schools not as test prep factories, but as active places for social change, and it envisions the leaders in them as moral agents practicing human agency. It is not a new idea for our schools. We find in our history figures such as George S. Counts, John Dewey, and many other far-thinking leaders who have had similar visions and ambitions to create a more just society by means of education.

In Conclusion

Aware of the history as related to the future of our public schools and of our commitment to prepare the leaders in them, we should acknowledge we will face the same assortment of opponents with the vested interests and agendas for retaining their own political power and social privileges as educators before us have faced. They will resist using the schools as levers for social change. Then as now, many find excuses for not acting. Then as now, we see legalisms used against us. Then as now, opponents claim changes cost too much. Then as now, we are told it's the victim's fault for not being motivated or intelligent. Then as now, we are told we aren't practical and are overly idealistic. Then as now, the struggle for justice, fairness and respect for all students continues.

Perhaps the most inspiring statement by any educational leader regarding a moral calling rooted in human agency was uttered by Horace Mann, the putative father of American public education who said in his last commencement address at Antioch College in Yellow Springs, Ohio, "Be ashamed to die until you have won some victory for humanity" (Fenner and Fishburn, 1944, p. 24). That's the best summing up there is.

PART 2

The Good, The Bad, and The Ugly: A Critical Review of Trends in Dissertation Research in Educational Administration/Leadership 2006–08

ROSEMARY PAPA and FENWICK W. ENGLISH

Introduction: The Ugly

> Good judgment comes from experience, and a lotta that comes from bad judgment. (Cowboy Way, 1998–2009)

The spaghetti western movie *'The Good, The Bad and The Ugly'* serves as a frame for Part II. Each section lends itself to some plain cowboy/girl euphuisms. Our book represents an effort at public engagement of scholars and practitioners in a renewed effort to redefine our field. In this part we examine thinking in the field of education administration as it is encapsulated in recent doctoral dissertations.

The dissertation is the recognized capstone of a potential leader's ability to engage in rigorous and creative thinking about practice. A review, presented here, of dissertation research undertaken from 2006 to 2008, reveals that there is much work to be done to improve the caliber of thinking in the preparation of educational administrators. It is our intention to frame the possibilities of expanding theoretical approaches in educational administration doctoral research with practices helpful to doctoral faculty and their students. Of significance for the field of educational administration is the constriction of dissertation research that continues to rely on stock theories and approaches.

Our research examined 1,027 doctoral dissertations in educational leadership completed during the time period 2006–08 as listed in ProQuest (2009). Based on a review of abstracts, 33% could be classified

47

as quantitative; 53% could be classified as qualitative and 12% as employing mixed methods. Two percent (2%) were classified as other. There was little variation in classifications across the three years of the study. Based on criteria advocated by proponents who seek to improve doctoral research, the authors undertook a more detailed analysis of six dissertations. In addition, we also examined the nature of the educational institutions producing dissertation research. That analysis revealed there has been a large increase in dissertation research at smaller more regional universities and colleges, and a huge jump in studies at for-profit, online universities.

The lack of quality of dissertation research in educational administration has become a favorite whipping boy of those convinced that educational leaders are being badly prepared to lead the kind of substantive reform that the schools appear to need. Levine's (2005) study of 28 schools of education criticized the research content as "superficial and lacking in rigor . . . confusing scholarly and practical inquiry, flitting from topic to topic, prizing breadth over depth, and being abstruse" (p. 44). He further stated,

> Educational administration scholarship is atheoretical and immature; it neglects to ask important questions; it is overwhelmingly engaged in non-empirical research; and it is disconnected from practice . . . [Research methodology was similarly berated as] poor for its over-dependence on qualitative methodologies, concentration on the descriptive, use of questionnaires of dubious reliability and validity, collection of data of questionable value, and inappropriate analysis of data (Levine, 2005, p. 44).

Levin (2006) similarly lamented that student dissertation research was undertaken mostly by part-time students who have taken only "low-level courses in research methods" (p. 40). As a result these part timers "learn more about replicating the language, imagery, and form of research than about the rigorous and systematic procedures that are necessary to produce defensible research results" (p. 40).

Archbald (2008) has indicated that criticisms of doctoral research have paid "little attention . . . to the powerful structures and values holding in place the traditional research dissertation" nor has it "examined the in-depth distinctions between research and organizational problem solving" (p. 704). He has proposed an alternative to the traditional research-based dissertation and defined it as a problem-based thesis.

These criticisms of doctoral programs are not new, though they have escalated in recent years, prompted by the agendas of right-wing think tanks that want to wrest public control of the schools away from current systems of governance and promote the privatization of both public schools and the leadership running them (Broad Foundation and Thomas B. Fordham Institute, 2003; Hess & Kelly, 2005). However, there are criticisms of doctoral programs from within the profession as well (see Miskel, 1988; Murphy & Vriesenga, 2004; National Commission on Excellence in Educational Administration, 1987). Our purpose is not to continue bashing the field, but to offer instructive criticism to better ourselves as a profession.

History of the Dissertation

Don't judge people by their relatives. (Cowboy Way, 1998–2009)

While there have been studies reported on the number of persons earning doctorates in educational administration who then enter the professoriate (Baker, Wolf-Wendel & Twombly, 2007), and subsequently the number of graduate degree programs and degrees granted in educational leadership (Baker, Orr, & Young, 2007), no studies have actually examined the numbers and types of dissertations completed in educational administration. It is our purpose to attempt to provide empirical evidence about the quantity and quality of recent dissertation research in educational administration/leadership.

While the Ph.D. in education was first granted by Teachers College, Columbia University in 1893, and Harvard University first awarded the Ed.D. in 1920, most close inspections show that in many universities there is little difference between the two degrees (Shulman, Golde, Bueschel & Garabedian, 2006, p. 25). For this reason we examined both Ed.D.s and Ph.D.s and subjected them to the same type of review.

Our review took place within a changing national degree-granting demographic, where some argue that lower status institutions are awarding more and more of the advanced degrees, while the Research 1 (former Carnegie Classification) institutions' share of the doctoral degree total is constant or shrinking (Baker, Orr & Young, 2007, p. 306). This is a troubling development since it means that the largest percentage of degree recipients will be graduating from "institutions that are less able to deliver a quality program, particularly quality doctoral programs" (Baker, Orr & Young, 2007, p. 306).

The designations have significantly changed since the Baker, Orr & Young, 2007 study. The designations are no longer limited to the single measure of funding, in that recent analysis considers both aggregate and per-capita measures of research activity. Because of these changes, the new categories are not comparable to those previously used, such as "Research I & II," etc. (Carnegie Foundation, 2007). The new designations are: (RU/VH Research Universities (very high research activity) and RU/H Research Universities (high research activity); DRU: Doctoral/Professions/Research dominant Universities (which include STEM and HSS); and SDE: Single Doctoral, Education. Carnegie Classifications (2007) are all-inclusive classifications and are time-specific snapshots of institutional attributes and behavior based on data from 2003 and 2004. Institutions might be classified differently using a different timeframe.

It is estimated that approximately 6,500 doctorates are awarded in education each year (Hoffer, Welch, Williams, Hess, Webber, K., Lisek, et.al, 2005). We examined both Ed.D. and Ph.D. dissertations listed through ProQuest (2009) between the years 2006 and 2008 in educational leadership (or approximately 1,027 of the total) posted through January 6, 2009. ProQuest is a database search engine that was used for researching the category 'Educational Leadership Dissertations.' In 1999, ProQuest was declared by the Library of Congress as the official U.S. off-site repository of digital dissertations. ProQuest categories relevant to our selection included:

- Educational leadership
- Educational leadership AND Higher education
- Educational leadership AND Colleges & universities
- Educational leadership AND College presidents
- Educational leadership AND School administration
- Educational leadership AND Awards & honors
- Educational leadership AND Personal profiles
- Educational leadership AND School principals
- Educational leadership AND Professional development
- Educational leadership AND Teachers
- Educational leadership AND Learning
- Educational leadership AND Students
- Leadership
- Leadership AND Educational services
- Leadership AND Public television
- Leadership AND Accreditation

Our review also revealed an increase in the number of doctoral dissertations among the for-profit, largely online degree university programs (Capella, Fielding Graduate, Walden, Regent, etc.) where full-time, research-productive faculty are not usually employed. Our data show there has been a shift in the total market share of production centers for dissertation research which is indicative of a profound change occurring on the degree and dissertation landscape.

The Review Criteria

Timing has a lot to do with the outcome of a rain dance. (Cowboy Way, 1998–2009)

A variety of criteria have been proposed to determine the quality of research in educational leadership. First, a task force of AERA scholars recommended that research in educational administration ought to:

1. present new knowledge to its audience;
2. be relevant to identifying, analyzing, and solving significant educational problems;
3. provide appropriate warrants for its assertions and conclusions;
4. be relevant to identifying, analyzing, and solving significant educational problems;
5. and be communicated effectively to its primary audience (Riehl, Larson, Short & Reitzug, 2000).

Levin (2006) posed six questions he believed would help the field address its most pressing problems. They were:

1. What are the most significant educational leadership issues, and why?
2. What conceptual models are most promising for addressing these issues through research?
3. How do we integrate the fields of educational policy and teaching and learning into research on educational leadership?
4. How do we train competent researchers to apply these methods to educational leadership issues?
5. How can we translate educational research effectively into useful guidelines for educational practice?
6. How can we establish expert panels or other oversight mechanisms to monitor, for quality assurance, research and training in the field of educational leadership? (p. 43).

In the following analysis we utilized the following criteria for examining the quality of dissertation research in educational administration/leadership:

1. Explicit Theoretical Grounding

We believe that a quality dissertation must be conceptually grounded in an explicit theoretical perspective. While we recognize that "chance discoveries" often occur outside theories, and some critics, including the authors, have argued that "canonical theoretical frameworks" may actually "limit vision, preserve the status quo, and prevent the kinds of eruptions of insight that tend to characterize knowledge growth in most fields," (Thomas, 1997, pp. 99–100), we also agree with Louis Pasteur that "chance favors only the prepared mind" (The Quotations Page, 1994–2007). We agree that the use of explicit theories enables the researcher to be more aware of the field of vision in play in undertaking research, and thus the mind is "prepared" to understand what is and is not unique or different in both problem definition and inquiry. We also recognize that very exploratory research may not enjoy a well-defined field, differentiated terms, and other criteria we advance here. However, we submit that such inquiry is best pursued by experienced researchers who fully understand the limitations, as opposed to neophytes undertaking their very first formal study. In this case, our reading of some dissertations has convinced us that statements regarding not employing conceptually rigorous theoretical grounding for a study often amounts to a "mea culpa" for sloppy work passed off as rigorous. Dissertations containing a caveat regarding "limitations in the study" were in fact lamentably limited—with the explicit admission of deficiency (when it appeared) providing no magical cure.

The presence of conceptual boundaries and content is important in shaping researchable questions of inquiry, forming a defensible line of argument, and in interpreting results and understanding the implications of those results. We would also argue that researchers who have minimal or no understanding of theories in use are so much more likely to reinforce existing practices and thought in the field. In our examination of the dissertations we sampled we found no conceptual breakthroughs from "theory-free" research.

2. Differentiated, Defined Concepts and Terms

We contend as well that a quality piece of research is informed by a vocabulary and terminology that leads to conceptual and operational differentiation. Dissertations that employ mushy ideas and terms such as "emotional intelligence," "transformational leader," and other popular but vague nomenclature, normally produce vague conclusions. Examples, extracted from the titles of the over 1,000 dissertations studied, include: *stigma of disclosure, activation of social capital, god-centered Christian leadership, critical spirituality, conceptual competency, leading from the nexus, transformative experiences, inter-cultural virtual learning community, unlocking leadership,* etc. Terms of this type often end up serving as nothing more than a list of platitudes in which a large range of actions is possible. Terms that fail to separate good and poor practice are comparable to buzzword homiletics. We think here of the "good to great" phenomenon (Collins, 2001) or the earlier and highly quoted Peters and Waterman text (1982) *In Search of Excellence,* which employed faked data (Lieberman, 2001). We also decry the use of kitsch management books deployed as "theoretical lenses" to frame such studies. Examples are Gladwell's (2000) *Tipping Point,* or Johnson's (1998) *Who Moved My Cheese?* Few, if any, of these sources have been empirically validated. Many are written by former pastors and are filled with hyperbole and over-simplification of complex issues and amount to little more than exhortation and managerial tarot cards (see Samier, 2005).

3. Advances the Content and/or Boundaries of the Field

We looked for dissertation research that exhibited a solid grounding in the major models of inquiry that have come to form the significant metanarratives that have dominated research in educational administration. These "typologies" have shaped what researchers were allowed to think about and answered such questions as "what constitutes a legitimate kind of research" in the field (English, 1994, pp. 99–132; Crow & Grogan, 2005; Papa, 2004; Papa & Brown, 2007; Young & Lopez, 2005). We found very few such references in the dissertation research we examined. It is as if students and their faculty advisors were unconscious or unaware of the extent to which their modes of inquiry followed familiar or well-worn patterns.

Too often in the quantitative studies we examined, the dissertation researcher obtained a pre-developed survey of some sort, defined a population and a sampling plan, administered the survey, and described the results. There were few discussions indicating the historical grounding of such surveys and how they were the same or different from dozens which may have gone before or if there were any expectations that the results obtained would be different or significant in a predictable or important way. As documented by the work of Baker, Orr, & Young (2007), numerous faculty advising doctoral students are former superintendents who themselves may have little grasp of the historical modes of inquiry that have defined the intellectual and conceptual typography of our field, even though they may be aware of current issues and problems.

4. Rigorous Methods

We do not define methodological "rigor" as deriving from one single perspective. We believe that rigor is contextually contained within a given theoretical perspective and is interdependent with that perspective and context. We eschew elevating a discussion of methodology to a plane that is independent of the research undertaken and the questions being pursued. What is "rigorous" depends on such circumstances. A highly-defined qualitative study is every bit as good as a highly-defined quantitative study using complex statistical techniques, whereas a poorly conceived "interview of ten teacher leaders" is as poor an analysis as a 100-item instrument using 50 2nd grade teachers.

5. Has Strong Implications for Improving Practice

We aver that a good example of dissertation research should have strong implications for improving practice, if not directly then at least in modifying or shaping a field of understanding in which practice is embedded. Archbald (2008) has called this criterion a "community benefit" in that "It reflects the expectation that the culminating product of doctoral education should make a difference" (p. 708). This is the "so what" question? To have a strong possibility of impacting practice relates to a dissertation's generalizability and hence to the sampling plan employed. Most such studies would be quantitative in nature. For us, qualitative inquiry is most useful in creating improved understanding of the context of practice and coming to grasp how practices are conceptualized and employed by practitioners in specific educational settings.

For purposes of illustrating what we considered to be good and poor examples of dissertation research we now provide a detailed analyses and critique of a sample of studies completed in 2008 as listed in ProQuest (2009). We do so as experienced dissertation advisors who have worked in eight different institutional settings, public and private, ranging from small Comprehensive I institutions to Research 1 institutions in five different states over the last twenty years. We also have served as external third-party reviewers of dissertations conducted in English-speaking countries outside the U.S. In addition, we have both presented research papers at AERA, UCEA, and NCPEA, and have served as officers on the executive boards and committees of UCEA and NCPEA as well as past presidents of both organizations.

As experienced dissertation advisors we are keenly aware of the many limitations that bear upon both advisors and students in engaging in doctoral research. We know all too well the shortcomings, which have been cited in other critiques of doctoral programs (Baker, Orr & Young, 2007; Levin, 2006; Levine, 2005; Shulman, Golde, Bueschel & Garabedian, 2006). These range from inadequate course preparation in methodology; inadequate grounding in epistemological issues; a preponderance of part-time students who have little time or incentive to engage in deep or far-reaching conceptual or practical research; lack of practice before attempting a major research undertaking; doctoral advisors who either lack an understanding of the practice of administration in real educational settings or have no grasp of rigorous research methods or any knowledge of the major patterns of intellectual inquiry which have been utilized in thinking and researching in educational administration as a field (English, 2002; 2003; 2007; Murphy, 1999; 2006; Murphy & Vriesenga, 2004; Papa, 2008). True scholar practitioners are quite rare in our field for many reasons, and this shortage is not likely to change anytime soon (see Baker, Wolf-Wendel & Twombly, 2007, p. 215).

In addition, as Labaree (2003) has noted, the type of knowledge in educational settings presents a major problem for educational researchers:

> If we think of knowledge as ranging from hard to soft and from pure to applied, educational knowledge [is] both very soft and very applied. This knowledge is thoroughly soft because it is an effort to make sense of of the collective consequences of the actions of large numbers of willful individuals who are making decisions about teaching and learning within a complex and overlapping array of social systems in response to multiple and conflicting purposes. Under such circumstances of great complexity, vast scale, uncertain purpose, and open choice, researchers are unlikely to establish valid and reliable causal claims that can be extended beyond the particulars of time, place, and person. As a result, research claims in education tend to be mushy, highly contingent, and heavily qualified, and the focus is frequently more on description and interpretation than on causation (p. 14).

Any examination of the quality of dissertation research has also to be situated within the types and kinds of knowledge claims that exist prior to the research activity, and take into consideration the types of outcomes that can be realistically expected as a consequence. We have attempted to take such factors into account and we offer our investigation with those caveats in mind.

The Approach to Assessing Current Dissertation Research

Never approach a bull from the front, a horse from the rear, or a fool from any direction. (Cowboy Way, 1998–2009)

We examined the type of dissertation research conducted in the years 2006-08 gleaned from the abstracts as cited in ProQuest (2009). The results are shown in Table 1.

Table 1 describes the total number of dissertations completed as referenced by ProQuest (see earlier description).

The major methodologies found in the studies across the three years are also reported. For the year 2006, 330 (32%) dissertations were completed. For 2007, 421 (41%) of the dissertations were completed. And, for 2008, 276 (27%) were completed through January 6, 2009.

In analyzing the methodology used in the 1,027 studies, three styles were generally clear: Quantitative, Qualitative and Mixed (a combination of quantitative and qualitative). Quantitative methodology included quasi experimental designs as well as the collection of data in numeric form, analyzed by a variety of statistical means. Qualitative included methodologies such as case studies, historical, biographical, etc. As can be seen in Table 1, 341 (33%) were classified as Quantitative, 545 (53%) classified as Qualitative, and 121 (12%) classified as Mixed. Twenty dissertations (2%) were classified as Other. There was little variation across the three years of the study for the percentages of each methodology for each year.

Thus, about one third of all dissertations completed over the last three

TABLE 1 Methodological Classification of Dissertations 2006–2008 In Educational Leadership.

Methodology	***2008	2007	2006	Totals
Quantitative	93	143	105	**341**
Qualitative	134	232	179	**545**
*Mixed	44	40	37	**121**
**Other	5	6	9	**20**
Totals	**276**	**421**	**330**	**1027**

*Mixed = A combination of both Quantitative and Qualitative methodology used.

**Other = Nature of abstract was unclear as to the methodology used
   Or summary of personal experiences
   Or developed curriculum
   Or position paper.

***2008 = Through January 6, 2009.

years were categorized as quantitative. Over half of all dissertations were classified as qualitative, and about an eighth were mixed methodology. Almost all Ed.D. and Ph.D. programs we've seen require graduate students to complete quantitative courses upon entry or at least during the core requirement phase. Presumably this is to better prepare candidates for reading as well as conducting statistically-based research. Yet, only about one-third actually conduct quantitative research.

Table 2 presents the universities and colleges used in this study categorized by Carnegie Classification (Carnegie Classification, 2007; The Chronicle, 2008). An institution was included if it produced greater than approximately 1% (n = 5 Ed.D. or n = 4 Ph.D.) of dissertations leading to either a Ph.D. or Ed.D.

As can be seen, the tables represent various types of colleges and universities including public, private, for-profit, large, small, religious based, etc., across the United States, Canada, England, South Africa, Sweden, Puerto Rico, Hong Kong and the Netherlands. The total number of Ph.D.s was 476 and the total Ed.D.s was 551.

It should be noted that the number of dissertations (n) leading to either the Ed.D. or Ph.D. are shown in Table 2. The percentages in the table are based on the total numbers Ed.D. (n = 551) and Ph.D. (n = 476).

TABLE 2 Degrees Awarded by Carnegie Classification.

Research Universities (Very High Research Activity)	**Ed.D.	n	**PhD.	n
Arizona State University	1%	8	1%	5
University of Arizona	1%	6		
University of Connecticut			1%	6
University of Delaware	1%	6		
Florida State University			1%	4
Harvard University	1%	6		
University of Illinois, Urbana Champaign			1%	5
Iowa State University				9
Kent State University			1%	4
University of Massachusetts, Amherst	1%	5		
Michigan State University			1%	5
University of Minnesota			1%	5
University of Nebraska, Lincoln			1%	5
New York University			1%	5
Ohio State University			1%	4
Oregon State University			1%	6

(continued)

TABLE 2 (continued) Degrees Awarded by Carnegie Classification.

Research Universities (Very High Research Activity) Continued	**Ed.D.	n	**PhD.	n
Pennsylvania State University, University Park			1%	7
Texas A&M University, College Station				10
University of California, Los Angeles			1%	4
University of Pennsylvania	3%	14	1%	5
University of Southern California	5%	30		
University of Texas, Austin	1%	6	2%	11
University of Virginia			1%	5
University of Wisconsin Madison			1%	7
All others less than 1% each	13%	71	16%	77
*Totals—24 institutions	28%	152	36%	173
Research Universities (High Research Activity)	**Ed.D.	n	**PhD.	n
Boston College			1%	7
Bowling Green University	1%	5		
University of Central Florida	1%	6		
University of Denver			1%	7
Drexel University			1%	4
Fordham University			1%	4
George Mason University			1%	5
George Washington University	2%	9		
Georgia State			1%	5
Indiana University, Bloomington			2%	8
University of Louisville			1%	7
Loyola University of Chicago			1%	5
Mississippi State University			1%	7
Northern Illinois University	1%	8		
Southern Illinois University at Carbondale			1%	6
Southern Mississippi			1%	4
Teachers College at Columbia University	2%	12		
University of Missouri, St. Louis	1%	5		
University of Ohio			11%	4
University of Nevada, Las Vegas			28%	4
University of New Mexico	1%	5		
All others less than 1% each	11%	58	11%	54
*Totals—21 institutions	20%	108	28%	131

(continued)

TABLE 2 (continued) Degrees Awarded by Carnegie Classification.

Doctoral/Professions/Research Dominant	**Ed.D.	n	**PhD.	n
Capella University			12%	57
Central Michigan University	1%	5		
Duquesne University	1%	6		
East Carolina University	3%	15		
Fielding Graduate University	2%	11		
Illinois State University	1%	6		
Indiana State University			2%	8
Indiana University, Pennsylvania	1%	6		
Pepperdine University	3%	16		
Regent University			2%	8
Seton Hall University	1%	7		
Spaulding University	1%	5		
Texas A&M University, Commerce	2%	10		
Union Institute & University			1%	6
University of Hartford	1%	5		
University of LaVerne	2%	10		
University of Phoenix Online Campus	3%	15		
University of San Francisco	1%	5		
Walden University			3%	15
All others less than 1% each	14%	79	7%	35
*Totals	**20%**	**201**	**27%**	**129**
S-Doc/Ed: Single Doctoral (Education)	**Ed.D.	n	**PhD.	n
University of the Incarnate Word			1%	6
Rowan University	2%	10		
Seattle University	1%	8		
Western Carolina University	1%	6		
Wilmington University	1%	5		
All others less than 1% each	9%	48	3%	17
*Totals—21 institutions	**14%**	**77**	**5%**	**23**

*Slight % discrepancies due to rounding error.
**% based on total Ed.D. and Ph.D. respectively.

It must be noted that the Carnegie Classification as shown in the *Chronicle* (2008) differs substantially from the more specific Carnegie Classifications shown on the Carnegie web pages (2009). For example, in the 2008 *Chronicle*, Doctoral/Research also includes universities that are shown as Doctoral Professional on their online resource. The institutions were included in the listed research categories only if they awarded at least 20 doctorates in 2003–4 (p. 34). Thus, we have listed these universities as Doctoral/Professions/Research dominant (which includes STEM and Humanities/Social Science doctoral institutions).

As can be seen for the Ed.D., the two Carnegie Classifications characterized as Very High and High Research Activity account for just under half of the Ed.D.s awarded. The category of Doctoral/Professions/Research Dominant accounts for a little over one-third of the Ed.D.s awarded. Within the Research Very High and High activity categories the University of Southern California led the way with 5% of total Ed.D. production.

That half of all Ed.D.s are awarded by Research Very High and High activity should hearten some of those in the field with respect to research and the Ed.D.

For the Ph.D., over sixty percent of degrees are awarded by the Research Very High and High activity designated universities. In these categories no single university was dominant.

What is noteworthy is that two universities in the Doctoral/Professions/Research Dominant category awarded 72 of the 129 Ph.D.s awarded. Capella University (an online program headquartered in Minneapolis) granted approximately 12% of *all* Ph.D.s awarded in the three years of the study. Walden University (another predominate online with some face-to-face) awarded an additional 3% of all Ph.D.s, with Regent University (originally founded by televangelist Pat Robertson) adding 2%, and Union Institute and University (a primarily distance education institution) adding an additional 1%. Thus, just under 20% of all Ph.D.s in Educational Leadership are awarded by online/non-traditional universities.

Academic and Institutional Production Centers

If you find yourself in a hole, the first thing to do is stop diggin'. (Cowboy Way, 1998–2009)

Baker, Orr & Young (2007) examined institutional production of graduate degrees from 1990 to 2003. They found that there had been a shift in the production of degrees by institutions in the U.S. While the total number of programs and degrees had substantially increased during the time period, there had been a shift in the type of institutions offering them. The older Carnegie classification of Research 1 programs, once the major production centers, had fallen dramatically, while there had been a four-fold increase in the production of degrees from comprehensive colleges and universities (p. 279). However, the emergence of the for-profit online university was not part of the Baker, Orr & Young (2007) study. Where Baker, Orr & Young reported that "comprehensive colleges and universities now exceed the doctoral degree production of the top 20 colleges of education [and therefore] . . . the pool of doctoral recipients is increasingly dominated by graduates from less selective institutions"(p. 296), our data show not only this trend but the heady rise of degree production by for-profit universities such as Capella and Walden.

The change in the production sites of advanced educational degrees in the U.S. has been called "academic drift" and has been prompted by two forces: (1) revenue-generating opportunities that had been left unexploited and (2) opportunities to advance institutional status on the academic food chain (Baker, Orr & Young, 2007, p. 306). Both of these are likely contributors to the rise of the for-profit online university. According to the *Almanac Issue* (2008–09) of *The Chronicle of Higher Education,* close to 45% of the four-year for-profit institutions have no application criteria at all compared to 13.7% for four-year private non-profits and 14.2% of the four year public institutions. Being less selective on admissions, as cited by Baker, Orr & Young (2007, p. 306), is a factor in the rise of degree production at for profit and online institutions. If the trends noted in our data continue, these degree programs will account for an increasingly larger segment of the total number of degree recipients. If that it the case, it follows that a higher proportion of school leaders and even future professors will be prepared by less selective educational institutions. We think the emergence of these production sites signals the beginning of a profound shift on the educational degree production landscape and we devote attention to it later.

Academic Drift or Academic Riptide? The Bad?

It don't take a genius to spot a goat in a flock of sheep. (Cowboy Way, 1998–2009)

The term "academic drift" is a misnomer. It is more like an academic riptide. *The New York Times* (Dillon, 2006) headlined the congressional decision to give for-profit online colleges federal student aid. Previously, colleges were required under federal student aid regulations to deliver over half their courses on a campus site. Taking the tack of better serving the nontraditional student, the Bush administration supported giving federal dollar support offering greater choice to students and primarily boosted the commercial education industry. For-profit enterprises vigorously pursued Republicans for this change. In 2006 the revenues of several for-profit higher education companies were cited in *The New York Times* article as exceeding $5.5 billion. These included the Apollo Group (University of Phoenix), Career Education Corp. and Education Management Corp. The rationale offered for the student aid decision by its proponents was that the more highly educated citizens earn higher salaries and thus pay more taxes back to society.

Online education had its genesis in providing canned programs. In order to mass produce courses information had to be "chunked" into clusters of related information. Entire books, for example, are condensed and woven into broader knowledge strands. The University of Phoenix, the nation's largest on-line university, offers a standardized curriculum that it owns. In most traditional universities the professors own the curriculum and are responsible for its content, accuracy, and currency. This shift was noted by *The Economist* (2005) when it wrote, "For-profit universities are only the most dramatic example of a more general trend: the changing balance of power between the state and the market" (Higher Ed Inc., p. 19).

Onsite preparation programs, as we have seen, have not been spared. For example, Murphy (2006b, March, p. 490), called "schools of education . . . slowstepping elephants when it comes to leadership education— sluggishly adjusting to today's call for new blood, stronger content, more relevance, and higher quality." He believed that deregulating higher education administration programs was superior to what exists today. But the implication exists that public and private non-profit universities may be unable to outrun the market of for-profit universities. If that is the case, the "traditional" programs could become irrelevant in the decades ahead. We believe not.

A capitalistic institution can increase revenues by being less selective or even non-selective regarding its customer. We distinguish between knowledge production and information reproduction and therein lies the value of the traditional university. Information reproduction began in the early 1990s with a rush to standardize our programs. A spur to that rush was NCATE accreditation linked to measurable standards through the 150 ELCC dispositions. As these were applied, department faculty were often forced to provide evidence of content and skills in a way that duplicated the elements. Additionally, the ELCC standards required that different assignments be used to evidence the assessment measurements. Thus, even the assessment processes became defined and further narrowed the curriculum and miniaturized the knowledge base. Hess & Kelly (2005b) lamented that the online programs that could offer an alternative to traditional universities did not in fact do so.

Although the hallmark of these providers is convenience and affordability, due to their heavy use of distance learning and online learning delivery, it is unclear that their training is substantively different from traditional providers. Indeed, because these programs are focused on profitability, they have strong incentives to emulate traditional programs, abide by traditional licensure rules, and ensure that graduates have an easy time obtaining licensure from the state. (pp. 173–4)

What Hess & Kelly (2005) did not address is the fact that the knowledge base was trivialized and miniaturized for easy delivery. This has led to the creation of online programs featuring knowledge chunked with absolutely no experiential qualities to it. We argue that such instructional material is not knowledge but information only. And, NCATE accreditation in our field has helped all of this to happen. The online proliferation of doctoral degrees offered through web sites is anything but drift. It is more an academic riptide as our data (see Table 2) indicate.

To begin to assess the actual quality of the dissertations, we choose to read all of the dissertation abstracts shown in *ProQuest* for 2008 through October of that year. We grouped them by dominant methodology employed. Of the original 139 dissertation abstracts read from 2008, we found 70 (50%) could be classified as qualitative. Forty-five (32%) were quantitative, and 23 (17%) employed mixed-methods, that is, a utilization of both quantitative and qualitative approaches. The fact that the largest percentage were qualitative was not surprising for as Labaree (2003) has noted, ". . . qualitative research is well suited to the task of making sense of the socially complex, variable-rich, and context-specific character of education" (p. 14).

However, doing qualitative research *well* is quite another task, as our review indicated. From our examination, we found that too many qualitative studies were not well designed and often amounted to little more than forays into such highly personal and site-specific circumstances as to have almost no generalizability even when similar contexts could be argued to exist.

Some Examples of Dissertation Writing

There never was a horse that couldn't be rode; Never was a cowboy who couldn't be throwed. (Cowboy Way, 1998–2009)

Our purpose for this study was purely investigatory. In no case did we find the abstracts inaccurate, though they did not always include all pertinent details. Our motivation was to simply see what was out there. We made no predictions, but instead pursued research as Einstein stated best,

"If we knew what it was we were doing, it would not be called research, would it?" (Quote DB, 2009). As of early October 2008, only 144 of the 2008 dissertation abstracts were posted on *ProQuest*. Selections of the six abstracts/dissertations was done with no intent of differentiating institutional affiliation i.e., online v. traditional in Carnegie classification. This was an investigatory study. At the time of selection we were unaware of any systematic classifications that needed exploration. Our original interest for this review of abstracts was involved with a search for life story/biography abstracts. Given our findings and our attempt to describe them to the field, we suggest further study be done based on all levels of Carnegie descriptions and online v. traditional institutional affiliation.

Based on the criteria suggested by committees and experts, and our own experience, we scanned the abstracts for examples of distinctive dissertations, some of which looked quite good and others not, according to our criteria. We wanted to determine if those criteria really differentiated among the dissertations. All of the examples cited are from 2008, but we do not explicitly identify the institutions or the authors. Our purpose was not to embarrass anyone, but to sample the writing and judge the work. The names and institutions are available for substantiation if necessary. For an easy reference system we employed the longstanding and familiar public school A-F grading scale in assessing each dissertation included in this section.

The Good

Dissertation 1 (Ph.D. qualitative): *Portraits of four Latina/Chicana leaders from migrant farmworker backgrounds and their leadership narratives*

Explicit Theoretical Grounding = B
Differentiated, defined concepts and terms = B
Advances the content and boundaries of the field = B
Rigorous methods = B
Strong implications for improving practice = B

This study was completed at a private, parochial single doctoral/other institution in the Northwest. The theoretical framework for the research was Chicana feminist theory and the method was portraiture. The purpose of the study was to explore the ideas and life experiences that influenced four undergraduate Latina students from first-generation Mexican migrant farmworker backgrounds to pursue leadership roles throughout their educational careers. The significance of the study was that the voices of Latinas are seldom represented in the literature and this study would fill such a void. Another objective was to enhance the scholarly literature of women's experiences in the leadership area. Each of the four Latinas was described in nine categories: identity; family and migration; education; role in the family; family legacy; ideas of leadership; experiences that influenced her to be a leader; challenges and supports; and art representation of leadership.

The study revealed that all the Latinas had strong family bonds and their cultural heritage helped them emerge as leaders. The women were proud of who they were and their heritage. The sacrifices of their families imbued them with a sense of personal worth. As children of farm workers they all possessed a strong work ethic. The women were also "cultural brokers" in that they had to translate language content in English to their families. This was an early leadership role. While the women's parents did not speak English well, they encouraged their children to value education and supported them in reading books. The four Latinas defined leadership as being about doing the right thing with passion and vision and having a purpose to give to others; and in the process they developed themselves. In their view leadership was not about a position. Rather, it was a collective phenomenon.

The researcher made recommendations for schools, such as encouraging the construction of environments unique to the experiences of migrant children would be appreciated and valued as well as becoming sites where the idea of leadership as a way of being and living was promoted. In this sense leadership was not separated from culture and day-to-day lived experiences. Leadership was not an abstraction but a way of living life. And, as a way of living, it would be embedded throughout the school's curriculum.

There were 162 bibliographical references in this strong dissertation, of which thirty-two (20%) were from vetted research journals or refereed academic conferences. Only eight (5%) were web-based. Six (4%) were other doctoral dissertations. None of them were from online universities. There were no kitsch management texts in the bibliography.

Dissertation 2 (Ed.D. mixed methods): *Unpacking the preparation of exemplary school principals shows graduate work does make a difference*

Explicit Theoretical Grounding = B
Differentiated, defined concepts and terms = B
Advances the content and boundaries of the field = C
Rigorous methods = B
Strong implications for improving practice = B

This study investigated the background, training, and development of 39 award-winning school principals in an Eastern state. The investigator resided in a public research university (very high research activity) in the same state. An initial supposition of the study was that effective principals used lessons learned as a part of graduate coursework or relevant professional development. The study was aimed at discerning what training might lead to the replication of these effective school leaders, and what did the institutions that prepared them have in common.

A survey instrument was utilized adapted from the Stanford Educational Leadership Institute. An online survey mechanism using a Likert scale was used for respondents. Means and standard deviations were computed, as were 't' tests. The results indicated that the respondents were able to distinguish between management and leadership lessons. Management lessons were best learned through graduate course work and some short-term professional development. On the other hand, leadership and strategy were best learned through personal relationships, nurtured over time and a long-term (more than 20 hour) professional development program. Experience on the job was highlighted as a reliable road towards excellence.

The respondents indicated that effective graduate programs had a comprehensive and coherent program of study; program content that highlighted instructional leadership as well as leadership for school improvement; faculty who were former practitioners and knowledgeable in their field of expertise; learning in a cohort structure; the mix of theory and practice; application of case studies; and widespread opportunities to reflect on their experiences and development. The conclusions of the study helped differentiate where exemplary principals actually learned their craft and reaffirmed in part the importance of graduate education in acquiring the requisite management skills to lead successful schools.

In contrast to other dissertations reviewed, this dissertation utilized seventy-five bibliographical references of which fourteen (19%) were from research journals and research conferences such as AERA. Ten (13%) were citations pertaining to theoretically important work in educational administration and its history. Seven (9%) were web-based citations.

The Bad

Dissertation 3 (Ed.D. quantitative): *Managerial style and student outcomes aren't related*

Explicit Theoretical Grounding = C
Differentiated, defined concepts and terms = C

Advances the content and boundaries of the field = D
Rigorous methods = C
Strong implications for improving practice = D

This dissertation used measures of managerial style to determine if any particular style was a predictor of success on measures of academic success in a Western state. The researcher performed the study at a single doctoral public education institution. The researcher began by only using school districts ($n = 284$) attaining the highest possible rating on the state's academic excellence indicator system. All superintendents were contacted and 49% were finally included as data in the study. Superintendents were asked to complete a managerial-style questionnaire that listed various managerial "styles," such as affiliative, authoritative, coaching, coercive, democratic and pacesetting. A series of ANOVAs were performed to assess differences for managerial styles on the outcome measures selected. The survey instrument employed had been used in the private sector and was normed on 35,433 cases (16,916 managers and 18,517 employees) from sixteen different industries.

The results of the study showed that while the "coercive/authoritative" managerial style was the most dominant reported by superintendents in high-scoring pupil achievement districts, that there were no statistically significant differences among the possible managerial styles self-reported when correlated to measures of academic performance. The researcher concluded that the study did not support the notion of a relationship of managerial style to student performance and brought into question the validity of the accountability instrument. This did not refer to the survey instrument, which was never questioned, but to the academic excellence indicator system in use. In this case, the efficacy of the managerial style survey was assumed to be valid. The notions that the instrument was not appropriate for school systems, relationship of management to student outcome data in schools, or even the concept of managerial style were left unchallenged. What the researcher did was challenge the efficacy of student achievement indicators, which the study was never designed to test. However, the notion of managerial style as a concept was a legitimate part of the study and could have been queried.

References in this study numbered 74 citations, of which 42% were web based. No academic journals were referenced. Three dissertations were cited, all from public institutions which are Carnegie classified: Texas A&M Corpus Christi (Single/Doctorate/Education), University of South Dakota (Doctoral/Profession/Research dominant) and University of Denver (Research-High activity). While books constituted 28% of the total references, few were theoretically rigorous.

Dissertation 4 (Ed.D. mixed methods, quantitative/qualitative):
Working long hours increases job stress or administrators shouldn't
work so hard!

Explicit theoretical grounding = B
Differentiated, defined concepts and terms = B
Advances the content and boundaries of the field = F
Rigorous methods = C
Strong implications for improving practice = D

This dissertation was aimed at investigating the extent to which health practices of secondary school principals in an Eastern state impacted their self-efficacy as leaders. Self-efficacy was defined as a belief in one's capabilities and was related to longevity and hence to sustainability. The study involved 118 secondary school principals. The theoretical base for the study was Bandura's (1986) social cognitive theory. The research plan was implemented in two-phases. The first was quantitative and the second involved interviews. A questionnaire, which included demographic items, was modified to measure self-efficacy in school improvement. In addition questions from the U.S. Center for Disease Control and Prevention were modified for use. Correlations and 't' tests were employed to determine differences in health practices and self-efficacy.

The results of the study indicated that principals struggle to maintain healthy lives and healthy habits given the demands of their jobs, that sticking to school improvement efforts showed a negative relationship to maintaining a desirable weight, a negative relationship between job stress and life satisfaction existed, and those who embraced good health practices tended to remain calm in stressful situations. Finally, if a principal works longer hours, it makes it more difficult to incorporate healthy practices, such as daily physical activity. Among the many recommendations as an outcome of this study is that policies should be developed at the state and district level to support school leaders by enabling them to reach school improvement goals without compromising their personal health.

This study was unnecessary. It is a reiteration of what is already known about job stress and health factors. It added very little to improving practice in the field or to the knowledge base impacting school leadership.

This dissertation included a total of 73 references, of which 16 (22%) were web-based. However, there were also seven (10%) references to research journals and one refereed conference paper.

The Ugly

Dissertation 5 (Ed.D. quantitative): *Flawed sampling and mushy concepts will not improve practice*

This dissertation was completed by a researcher at an all online university with a web site in the West. It was concerned with performing a correlational study of servant leadership and elementary school principal job satisfaction in a mid-Western state where the researcher lived.

Our ratings for this dissertation were as follows:

Explicit Theoretical Grounding = C
Differentiated, defined concepts and terms = D
Advances the content and boundaries of the field = F
Rigorous methods = D
Strong implications for improving practice = F

The crux of this dissertation concerned whether or not in school districts determined via survey to have implemented servant leadership practices, elementary school principals possessed or exhibited greater job satisfaction. The researcher was an elementary principal.

The researcher had several difficulties in doing this study. The first was that the instrument utilized to determine the presence of servant leadership was filled with mushy concepts that lacked precision. For example, the servant leader was defined as doing such things as valuing people, building community, displaying authenticity, providing leadership, sharing leadership, etc. Clearly these attributes could be applied to almost any perspective with similar clusters, from Gandhi's nonviolent movement (ahimsa) to Buddhism or the late Edward Deming's (1993) fourteen points, which contained such admonitions as "be a good listener," "set an example," "continually teach people," "optimization for everyone," etc. (p. 95). The "servant organization" was defined as "an organization in which the characteristics of servant leadership are displayed through the organizational culture and are valued and practiced by the leadership and workforce." Furthermore, a review of the survey instrument revealed it was derived by employing a Delphi technique. Such a technique uses several rounds of polling to settle on the attributes of an entity, concept or idea.

The dilemma with using such an approach is one which Lakatos (1999b) has called the problem of "inductivism." It plagues much social science research and it is that "... a fact may not be used twice, first in the construction of the theory and subsequently in support of it" (p. 111). The result of such an approach is that by using the same facts twice (in the case of a Delphi program), facts are determined to be correlative to one another and descriptive of the whole. However, there is no independent measure possible to validate it outside the process itself. Lakatos (1999) notes that "the very notion of empirical support is heuristics-dependent" (p. 112), in this case descriptors for job satisfaction are simply a subset of those describing servant leadership. In this case it would have been surprising not to have "discovered" positive correlations.

The researcher stumbled on the sampling plan. To determine a district's approach to servant leadership, the researcher indicated that a random sample was derived from the 619 school districts in the state. Thus the school district was the sampling unit. For a probability level of 0.05 the sample size was determined to be around 30 by reference to a statistics text that indicated to the author that a sample should comprise at least 30 instances (we know of no such methodology).

The survey was then sent to 28 superintendents, of which 25 were received. The researcher then moved to sample the elementary principals and teachers in the same districts. However, there are 2,254 elementary schools in the same state not 619. So the district sampling unit was used for elementary principals. A question arises, is a random sample of school districts the same as a random sample of elementary school principals? For example, if the preponderance of school districts in the state are rural, but a preponderance of elementary school principals are urban because there are more schools in urban settings, is elementary principal job satisfaction actually a random determination?

The researcher discerned that the responses to the study's two questions were statistically significant, that is that public school districts were implementing the principles of servant leadership and that the level of servant leadership correlated with elementary principal job satisfaction. In arguing that the results showed that job satisfaction was an important factor in elementary principal job satisfaction and might be something to consider to keep principals from leaving their jobs, the same set of statistics gathered indicated that "the longer superintendents worked in their current position, the lower their job satisfaction was rated on the [survey]." Similarly among the overall respondents there was a significant negative correlation found between "total years in the field of education and years planned to continue working in the field of education."

This finding was reported among school systems that were ostensibly already using the principles of servant leadership. A questions such as the following was never explored, "If the principles of servant leadership are operational, why is it that their implementation is not enough to offset the negative effects of longitudinal service in the same systems?" There were no practical effects of this study for resolving any significant issue facing the field including that of administrative turnover. The dissertation concluded by noting, ". . . this study's findings indicated that servant leadership has merit to be studied further in public school settings."

The servant leadership dissertation contained ninety-two bibliographical citations. Of these 75% were web-based. There were no references to research vetted in a refereed journal or even a national research conference. Of the twenty-three dissertations cited, 43% were from other online universities (Capella, Regent, etc.) Only two dissertations were from research universities. The prior studies had no external review of their efficacy or quality before being utilized.

Dissertation 6 (Ed.D. qualitative): *The fallacy of revelatory knowledge as a data base*

This dissertation was completed in 2008 at a public Eastern Single Doctoral Education institution, meaning the only doctorate given at the institution was in education. The study was concerned with God-centered Christian spiritual leadership.

Our ratings for this dissertation were:

Explicit Theoretical Grounding = F
Differentiated, defined concepts and terms = D
Advances the content and boundaries of the field = F
Rigorous methods = F
Strong implications for improving practice = F

This dissertation was classified by its author as "autoethnography." The researcher was an elementary school principal who often prayed with parents and opened school ceremonies by honoring Jesus Christ even though he ran "the risk of being accused of not separating church and state." The researcher described "God-centered Christian spiritual leadership or GCCSL as not a theory, but "conceived by me, under the direction of the Holy Spirit, God-centered Christian spiritual leadership seeks to use the Bible and the leading of the Holy Spirit to affect the culture of an organization" The researcher also eschewed formal religion because of beliefs or practices found offensive and attacked the evils of secular humanism as "the idea of humankind being self-directed, self-centered and autonomous [that has its] roots in an educational system that has sought to lead its disciplines down a road paved with logic and guided by a scientific methodological approach." The writer used the technique of journaling to "support the notion of a God-centered Christian Leadership approach that is predicated on a relationship with God, rather than religious practices and rituals." The journal entries were then used as "data" to justify the researcher's own predilections and suppositions as a practitioner of the religious viewpoint espoused. In stipulating the choice of autoethnography the researcher said, "I will explore these and other questions as I conduct an autoethnography of my leadership and its grounding in my belief and relationship with my Lord and Savior, Jesus Christ."

In his Chapter 5, the researcher noted that "the journal also included what is called in Christianity 'revelation knowledge;' knowledge considered by the individual as being too profound to have come out of their cognitions and believed to be divinely inspired." Not only is such knowledge not of the earthly kind but it is divinely inspired to be out of reach and out of verification in the usual scientific channels.

There were fifty-three total bibliographical references in this dissertation. There were no references to empirical research from educational or research journals, and only seven references (13%) to serious academic journals such as *The Journal of American History, Educational Administration Quarterly* (one reference), or the *Educational Researcher* (one reference). Of the books cited, twelve (22%) were what Samier (2005) has called "kitsch" management texts. Such texts are not research-based. The definition of "kitsch":

> requires no knowledge, understanding, critique, or analysis; It is predigested and pre-packaged, sparing effort and providing a short-cut to pleasure. Its appeal . . . lies in the following principles: it is easily understood, satisfies an immediate desire, does not disturb or challenge basic sentiments and beliefs, does not question socio-political reality or vested interests, it reinforces our prejudices, avoids unpleasant conflicts, and promises a happy ending . . . Translated into administrative or managerial terms, it is the promise of a painless, effortless, and conflict-free path to organizational improvement (Samier, 2005, p. 38).

Examples of kitsch management books cited in this dissertation were *Grace-full leadership: Understanding The Heart of a Christian Leader* (Bowling, 2000); *Synchronicity: The Inner Path of Leadership* (Jaworksi, 1996) and *The Purpose Driven Life* (Warren, 2002). Not surprisingly we found no data at all to support the following assertions proposed by the researcher in this dissertation:

1. "With their label and self-fulfilling prophecy in hand, they [the usual sort of leader schooled in traditional leadership theories found in universities] go forth and attempt to make a difference only to discover that they contradict their professed leadership style so often that they begin to feel as though they are in a state of leadership schizophrenia."

2. "It is the educators in the aforementioned educational climate that are perplexed by the fact that with all of the data at their disposal, a myriad of available curricula, and laws demanding accountability, there is a large segment of our student population on the cusp of being disenfranchised. Having compromised the throne of educational supremacy, America is scrambling to maintain a semblance of its economic supremacy in a global village that uses education as its weapon of mass economic destruction."

3. "Without God, humankind reverts to a level of selfishness that is, at best, cold and uncaring, and could lead to self-destruction."

We found this dissertation, for which an Ed.D. was awarded at a public university, an egregious misuse of the scientific process in which the researcher when conducting his literature review contended that "Scripture, believed to be the divinely inspired word of God by the GCCSL, must take precedence over the work of scholars." Epistemologically the study grounded its "findings" not on any empirical data, but instead on notations of practices grounded in solipsism and praying on school premises. There can be no true investigation of any kind within this framework. There can be no empirical or scientific study in which personal faith trumps public findings.

Here one can recall the admonition of Pierce (1955) as to why faith cannot be the basis of certainty. First, humans can never really be sure that any given claim is actually warranted. Secondly, assertions grounded in faith cannot be supported by reasoning. Third, the foundation of faith can never be established as ultimately true because revelation "far from affording us any certainty, gives results less certain than other sources of information" (p. 57).

What the Dissertations Reveal

Lettin' the cat outta the bag is a whole lot easier than puttin' it back. (Cowboy Way, 1998–2009)

Our analysis of these dissertations revealed the following. We hope these preliminary findings will spur additional reviews and analyses.

1. Strong Dissertations Are Complex Products

The quality of a dissertation is connected to the use of vetted prior research, solid theoretical grounding, and rigorous methods. Dissertations that manifested these elements had fewer web-based citations and made more use of refereed data sources and books that were theoretically rigorous. The extensive citation of prior dissertations, which were never vetted in referred publications, generally signaled a weaker product. A huge number of web-based citations could signal that the researcher had rarely set foot in a library, still a standard for thoroughness in approaching a topic. Similarly a large number of "kitsch" or "pop-management" citations is usually a sign that the terms to be used in a study lack precision and the thinking behind them is intellectually flawed.

2. Rigor Is More than Method

Too often rigor is simply thought of as the use of advanced statistics or in qualitative research "thick descriptions." But method alone cannot produce quality. If terms are ambiguous and the theoretical base weak, sophisticated methods cannot transform the studies using such terms or theory into quality pieces of work. In short, there is no remedy for a theoretically weak or trivial topic. Method does not by itself entail value or quality.

3. Practicality In a Dissertation is Connected to Risk

Whether a study is of value to the field depends upon how well the researcher understands the intellectual topography in which a study is located. A risky study is one which involves elements of great uncertainty and conjecture, but one in which the unknown is significant and can be described on the conceptual and intellectual terrain. What this means is that a researcher needs to have a good understanding of the context and also have something significant to explore. We note here that Kamler and Thomson (2008, November) found in their review of dissertation advice books that in general these texts offered "urban myths about research and oversimplified rules and lists" that preclude problem-solving at the intended "highest level of scholarship" (p. 511).

Cookie-cutter approaches by either students or professors who use dissertation how-to manuals in 'research orientation courses' or doctoral seminars encourage a low level of thought among students. Studies with very low risk signal that the topic is well-worn and the potential to impact the field is very low or negligible, because the veins of discovery are too well mapped and mined.

We also note that risk has another dimension, that is, the road the student takes to defining a topic in working with his/her advisor and doctoral committee. We have reason to believe that conservatism usually prevails. That means that when a topic or approach is being considered, there is a strong tendency to avoid controversy and contention and select topics where a great deal of study has already occurred. This makes the literature review much easier and increases the comfort level of all parties. But it also increases the probability that what may be learned will be trivial. We would rather see important topics tackled with greater ambiguity, even with some study flaws, than in reproducing the already discovered with great precision.

4. Implications for Advancing the Field Will Require New Methodologies

If doctoral research is to be judged on whether or not it improves or has the capability of advancing the field, such an expectation will require stronger methodologies than are typically found in most doctoral programs we know. In the typical program it is the student who selects a topic and seeks out advisors to assist him/her in the process. Many doctoral advisors are loath to interfere in the process very much except perhaps to decline to serve based on expertise or even interest. This stance may have to change. Too often what students want to study is so reduced in scope or importance that it renders significant findings moot, positive or negative. Students rarely understand where the boundaries of a field are located and too many advisors are similarly confused. Improving the capacity of doctoral research to change our field simply cannot be left to student or any single advisor's discretion. We believe that to ensure that doctoral research is not "irrelevant, silly, superficial or contorted" (Clifford & Guthrie, 1988, p. 336) will require new methodologies that raise the level of awareness that any potential topic must have real potential to effect change. Not developing novel methodologies means accepting that educational doctoral dissertations will continue to reproduce failed strategies.

Improving Doctoral Research: Avoiding Knee Jerk Solutions

Inscription on John Wayne's headstone: "Tomorrow is the most important thing in life. Comes into us at midnight very clean. It's perfect when it arrives and it puts itself in our hands. It hopes we've learnt something from yesterday." (Cowboy Way, 1998–2009)

Part I documented the rise of more convenient and easier preparation programs, which are not indexed to measures of quality. Our research reveals the rise of the online university and its online degrees as a potential "game changer" for preparation programs, providing even less incentive for true paradigmatic work that runs against the grain of current thinking.

Based on our review of the abstracts of 1,027 doctoral dissertations at 251 institutions or online production centers for 2006–08 in the United States and abroad and a close reading of selected dissertations, we could not find any that were exemplars of spectacular new breakthroughs in educational leadership. There were no "penicillin" discoveries in what we read. Prima facie this is disappointing, since one of the purposes of research is to create new knowledge and extend the boundaries of current knowledge. What we read were mostly refinements of existing practices and thought within well- trodden paths of inquiry. Perhaps this dimension is simply unattainable for doctoral research since it is often the first (and last) original research done by most graduates. Students have not mastered the research act and in our work with colleagues too many graduate advisors prefer the familiar topics and approaches over anything radically different. It is not hard to understand that the price of respectability is too often conservatism of thought.

This problem is not confined to educational administration. Adams and White (1994) examined doctoral research in public administration in 1992 and found:

> 24% were not guided by any theoretical or conceptual framework; 37% had obvious design flaws; 46% contributed nothing to knowledge development in the field, having no theoretical relevance; 33% appeared to have no practical relevance; 36% addressed unimportant topics in the field; 49% were under 250 pages in length; 13% used qualitative methods and only 5% were theoretical and 10% historical.

Adams and White (1994) summarized their assessment by noting that "the field is a theoretical wasteland, subject to mindless empiricism and parochialism."

If another field of administrative practice has also suffered from the same problems as educational administration, we ought to pause before jumping to any "knee jerk" solutions. For example, we disagree with Levin (2006) that what educational administration research needs is "more" rigor, less qualitative research, and no discussions regarding epistemology or ontology. We believe, rather, that our notion of "science" is at the root of our problem. That notion has miniaturized our field. Eliminating the humanities and aesthetics from educational administration inquiry (Ribbins, 2006) has reduced its scope and with it any full understanding of the nature of leadership (see Greenfield & Ribbins, 1993; Heilbrunn, 1996; Samier, 2005; Young & Lopez, 2005; English 2008).

The history of the field of educational administration has been one in which the intellectual founders were intent on finding a science amidst the narratives of practice (Crow & Grogan, 2005; Culbertson, 1988; Donmoyer, 1999; Greenfield & Ribbins, 1993; Papa, 2004). This prevailing mentality has very deep roots in the intellectual soil of the academe today. When the science one uses to seek deeper understandings of the world of practice imposes reduced contextual requirements, what it inevitably produces are simplicisms and superficialities. This penchant is still very much regnant in the continuing quest for measurability, quantifiability, traits, behaviors, rubrics, categories, typologies, taxonomies and all the other accoutrements of positivistic science that remain embodied in accreditation standards, certification requirements, and dissertations. We are reminded of Heilbrunn's (1996) admonition about leadership studies:

> The mystery of leadership touches on some of the more vexing philosophical questions about human existence, which theorists ignore only at the risk of ultimate irrelevance . . . the most important things about leadership lie far beyond the capabilities of science to analyze (p. 11).

For us, the solution to producing improved doctoral level research isn't requiring more courses in quantitative analytical methods or authorizing only research that includes clinical field trials as advocated by the National Research Council (2002). Rather it means going back and redefining the nature of knowing and the phenomenon of leadership on a restored landscape of intellectual and contextual complexity. It means coming to terms with the limitations of the behavioral sciences and penetrating the curtain with which these same sciences enshroud the study of leadership.

To that end we see improved doctoral level research being played out by substantive changes in the courses typically found in educational leadership curricula. The curriculum must move beyond the usual personnel, law, collective bargaining, finance, organizational theory pre-requisites to include courses in history, the humanities, the arts, dimensions of the aesthetic, ethics, biography and as T.B. Greenfield and Ribbins (1993) noted long ago, theology and philosophy. Without such substantive changes we will continue to produce the kinds of dissertations we found dominant in our analyses. Greenfield and Ribbins (1993) predicted such a result when he said:

> The cost of this development [the theory movement and positivistic science] is that enquiry becomes disparate, disjointed, and noncumulative. Virtually any topic is good enough. The field as a field of study begins to disappear (p. 219).

We see in the proliferation of programs and dissertation research in the expansion of doctoral studies (and in the new completely online programs and the dissertations they produce) a new intellectual orthodoxy and the enclosure of the field of inquiry within the processes of standardization and within a model of science that has decapitated leadership in the guise of seeking to improve it. It is indeed a cruel paradox that what we sought to discover we effaced in the act of discovery.

While we are not without solutions to these dilemmas, the barriers to implementing them are formidable, e.g., relaxation of mandates, attenuated accreditation and the realities of the profits of the marketplace being yoked by the new purveyors in the information/knowledge industry for asynchronous "anytime" study. These are very powerful forces. But the first step is to acquire an accurate picture of where we are now and the issues and problems to be confronted in improving dissertation research. Our pivotal tenet echoes Greenfield and Hodgkinson's (Greenfield & Ribbins, 1993) admonition of many years ago that, "The central questions of administration are not scientific but philosophic" (47). If that is the case, and we have no reason to believe otherwise, one would expect to see a discernible shift in the types and kinds of dissertations completed in the time period of our study. However, our data suggests that the vast majority of professors advising doctoral students would not agree, and that our field remains firmly in the grasp of the notions of administrative science, no matter how unproductive or intellectually discredited or barren it may have become.

A Comment for The Good

Courage is being scared to death—and saddling up anyway. (Cowboy Way, 1998)

We began Part 2 with the intention to frame the possibilities of expanding theoretical approaches in educational administration doctoral research in practices helpful to doctoral faculty and their students. Of significance for the field of educational administration is the constriction of dissertation research that continues to rely on stock theories and approaches. As we have stated, the history of the field of educational administration has been one in which the intellectual founders were intent on finding a science amidst the narratives of practice (Crow & Grogan, 2005; Culbertson, 1988; Donmoyer, 1999; Greenfield & Ribbins, 1993; Papa, 2004). The crucial term here is "science." When the science one uses to seek deeper understandings of the world of administrative practice imposes reduced contextual requirements, what it inevitably produces are simplicities and superficialities. If the science as applied is limited, the results will be similarly limited. In training administrators, professors must be conscious of the multiple meanings of science.

We offer a number of practical ideas to our fellow colleagues on helping students see and appreciate more than the "stock" theories and approaches. Our manifesto for the field of education leadership focuses on how we actively perform our research. We conclude with our thoughts for doctoral students in our field.

1. Use explicit theoretical grounding within an epistemocratic conduit.

    A quality dissertation must be conceptually grounded in an explicit theoretical perspective. That perspective must be located within an epistemocratic framework or conduit as shown in Figure 5. The epistemocratic conduit is a construct with historical underpinnings. A doctoral student should be able to sketch out the history of the epistemocratic conduit in which his/her study is to occur.

2. Understand the need for differentiated, defined concepts and terms.

    A quality piece of research is informed by a vocabulary and terminology that leads to conceptual and operational differentiation. Dissertations that employ mushy ideas and terms often end up serving as nothing more than a list of platitudes in which a large range of actions is possible. Students should try to avoid titles with variables such as emotional intelligence; stigma of disclosure; activation of social capital; critical spirituality, etc

3. Ensure your focus advances the content and/or boundaries of the field.

    Ask yourself, "What will your study add to the body of knowledge in the field?" Define the solid grounding through understanding and providing evidence of the major models of inquiry that have come to form the significant metanarratives that define our field.

4. Select rigorous methods that make sense to your study.

    What is "rigorous" depends on such circumstances. A highly defined qualitative study is every bit as good as a highly defined quantitative study using complex statistical techniques.

5. Express the strong implications for improving practice.

    Good dissertation research should have strong implications for improving practice, if not directly then at least in modifying or shaping a field of understanding in which practice is. This is the 'so what' question?

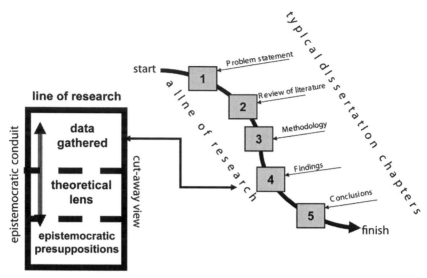

FIGURE 5 An Illustration of a Line of Research within an Epistemocratic Framework.

So, while we agree with Archbald (2008) that it is time to come to terms with these issues in conducting doctoral research in educational leadership, we do not concur that a split in the focus of the kinds of dissertation is a desirable alternative because one is less theoretical than the other. We see that line of argument as promoting a false dichotomy between theory and practice which has been discredited by Lakatos' (1999) progressive-regressive research programs continuum concept. Deming (1993) perhaps said it best:

> To put it another way, information, no matter how complete and speedy, is not knowledge. Knowledge has temporal spread. Knowledge comes from theory. Without theory, there is no way to use the information that comes to us on the instant (p. 109).

We propose a line of research as shown in Figure 5 rests within a conduit of epistemocratic presuppositions. The entire delineation of the chapters in the traditional dissertation (which we are not necessarily defending but describing) are contained within this conceptual/epistemocratic pipeline. A cut-away view of the conduit shows at the base the often unstated and/or unknown epistemocratic presuppositions at work in pursuing a specific line of research. These presuppositions influence the selection of a theoretical lens through which subsequent data are gathered. Data must conform to the epistemocratic presuppositions and to the boundaries of the theoretical lens employed. No study can examine everything. The epistemocratic conduit enables research to be manageable, but it also contains the danger of overlooking fugitive information which was not expected and which falls outside the conduit.

It is at this critical juncture that the difference between verification and discovery described in Part 1 often hinges. We believe that too few of our graduate students have a sufficient theoretical and historical view of past thinking and practices in our field to adequately separate them. And too many are rushing through this aspect of their doctoral work, treating the research requirement as a *pro forma* exercise to be completed as rapidly as possible and with the least amount of serious attention to the entire research act. Too few have developed a deep appreciation as to how their thinking about conducting inquiry has been pre-shaped by the often unconscious acceptance of the epistemocratic presuppositions, which determine not only the size of the conduit but what is permissible within it.

From this vantage point, most doctoral research is not too theoretical, but not theoretical enough. A failure to distinguish such differences dooms dissertations to be representations of shallow thinking devoid of the intellectual/conceptual positioning necessary to change practice which will lead to substantive improvements in the schools. We think it is time to step back and reconsider the scope and meaning of doctoral research in doctoral programs. It is upon this pivotal point that the many meanings of "research rigor" can be contemplated. That must include scope, depth, content and methods situated in contexts of practice and thought that restore the human in all its manifestations.

References

Ackerman, R. & Maslin-Ostrowski, P. (2002). *The wounded leader: How real leadership emerges in times of crisis.* San Francisco: Jossey-Bass.

Adams, G. & White, J. (1994). Dissertation research in public administration and cognate fields: An assessment of methods and quality. *Public Administration Review, 54*(6), 565–576.

Allison, D. (1999). Structuralism. In R. Audi (Ed.) *The Cambridge dictionary of philosophy, 2nd Ed.* Cambridge, UK: Cambridge University Press, 882–4.

Anderson, G. & Pini, M. (2005). Educational leadership and the new economy: Keeping the "public" in public schools. In F. English (Ed.) *The SAGE handbook of educational leadership* (pp. 216–236). Thousand Oaks, CA: SAGE.

Archbald, D. (2008, December). Research versus problem solving for the educational leadership doctoral thesis: Implications for form and function. Educational *Administration Quarterly, 44* (5), 704–739.

Argyris, C. (1972). *The applicability of organizational sociology.* London: Cambridge University Press.

Armstrong, K. (2005). *A short history of myth.* Edinburgh: Canongate.

Baker, B., Orr, M. & Young, M. (2007, August). Academic drift, institutional production, and professional distribution of graduate degrees in educational leadership. *Educational Administration Quarterly,* 43 (3), 279–318.

Baker, B.D., Wolf-Wendel, L. & Twombly, S. (2007, April). Exploring the faculty pipeline in educational administration: Evidence from the survey of earned doctorates, 1999–2000. *Educational Administration Quarterly,* 43 (2), 189–220.

Bandura, A. (2001). Social cognitive theory: An agentive perspective. *Annual Review of Psychology,* 52, 1–26.

Bandura, A. (1986). *Social Foundations of thought and action: A social cognitive theory.* Englewood Cliffs, NJ: Prentice-Hall.

Bates, R. (2006). Towards an aesthetics for educational administration. In E. Samier & R. Bates (Eds.) *Aesthetic dimensions of educational administration and leadership* (pp. 205–220). London: Routledge.

Berman, B. (1983, Fall). Business efficiency, American schooling, and the public school superintendency: A reconsideration of the Callahan thesis. *History of Education Quarterly,* 23, 297–321.

Beveridge, W. (1950). *The art of scientific investigation.* New York: Vintage Books.

Blackbourn, J. (2006). Behaviorism. In F. English (Ed.). *Encyclopedia of Educational Leadership and Administration.* Thousand Oaks, CA: Sage, 703.

Blasé, J., & Blasé, J. (2003). *Breaking the silence: Overcoming the problem of principal mistreatment of teachers.* Thousand Oaks, CA: Corwin Press.

Bloom, H. (1998). *Shakespeare: The invention of the human.* New York: Riverhead Books.

Bloomfield, L. (1933). *Language.* New York: Holt.

Blount, J. (2008). History as a way of understanding and motivating social justice work in education. In T. Townsend and I. Bogotch (Eds.) *Radicalizing educational leadership: Dimensions of social justice* (pp. 17–38). Rotterdam: Sense Publishers.

Blount, J. (2005). *Fit to teach: Same-sex desire, gender, and school work in the twentieth century.* Albany: State University of New York Press.

Blount, J. (1998). *Destined to rule the schools: Women and the superintendency, 1873–1995.* Albany: State University of New York Press.

Blumberg, A. (1989). *School administration as a craft: Foundations of practice.* Needham Heights, MA: Allyn and Bacon.

Bogotch, I. (2008). Social justice as an educational construct. In T. Townsend & I. Bogotch (Eds.). *Radicalizing educational leadership: Dimensions of social justice* (pp. 79–112). Rotterdam: Sense Publishers.

Bolman, L. & Deal, T. (1991). *Reframing organizations.* San Francisco, CA: Jossey-Bass.

Bolton, C. & English, F. (2009). My head and my heart: De-constructing the historical/hysterical binary that conceals and reveals emotion in educational leadership in E. Samier and M. Schmidt (Eds.) *Emotional dimensions of educational administration and leadership* (pp. 125–142). Abingdon, UK: Routledge.

Born, D. (1996). Leadership studies: A critical appraisal. In P. Temes (Ed.) *Teaching leadership: Essays in theory and practice* (pp. 45–72), New York: Peter Lang.

Bottery, M. (2004). *The challenges of educational leadership.* London: Paul Chapman.

Bourdieu,P. (2001). *Firing back: Against the tyranny of the market 2.* New York: The New Press.

Bourdieu, P. (1998). *Acts of resistance: Against the tyranny of the market* (R. Nice, Trans.) New York: The New Press.

Bourdieu, P. (1984). *Distinction: A social critique of the judgment of taste.* R. Nice, trans. Cambridge, MA: Harvard University Press.

Bourdieu, P. (1977). *Outline of a theory of practice.* R. Nice (trans.). Cambridge: Cambridge University Press.

Bourdieu, P. & Passeron, J-C. (2000). *Reproduction in education, society and culture, 2nd ed.* London: Sage.

Bowles, S. & Gintis, H. (1976). *Schooling in capitalist America: Educational reform and the contradictions of economic life.* New York: Basic Books.

Bowling, J. (2000). *Grace-full leadership: Understanding the heart of a Christian leader.* Kansas City, MO: Beacon Hill Press.

Bremmer, I. (2009, May–June). State capitalism comes of age: The end of the free market. *Foreign Affairs,* 88 (3), 40–55.

Broad Foundation and Thomas B. Fordham Institute (2003). *Better leaders for America's schools: A manifesto.* Retrieved February 11, 2004, from http://www.edexcellence.net/doc/Manifesto.pdf.

Callahan, R. (1962). *Education and the cult of efficiency.* Chicago: University of Chicago Press.

Campbell, J. (1973). *The hero with a thousand faces.* Princeton, NJ: Princeton University Press.

Campbell, R., Fleming, T., Newell, L. & Bennion, J. (1987). *A history of thought and practice in educational administration.* New York: Teachers College Press.

Caplan, B. (2007). *The myth of the rational voter: Why democracies choose bad policies.* Princeton, NJ: Princeton University Press.

Carnegie Classification. (2007). *Classification descriptions.* Retrieved on January 25, 2009 from: http://www.carnegiefoundation.org/classifications/index.asp?key=785.

Carnegie Foundation. (2007). *Graduate instructional program description.* Retrieved on December 14, 2008 from: http://www.carnegiefoundation.org.index.asp.

Caro, R. (2002). *The years of Lyndon Johnson: Master of the senate.* New York: Knopf.

Carnoy, M., Jacobsen, R., Mishel, L. & Rothstein, R. (2005).*The charter school dust-up: Examining the evidence on enrollment and achievement.* New York: Economic Policy Institute and Teachers College Press.

Cherryholmes, C. (1988). *Power and criticism.* New York: Teachers College Press.

Chronicle of Higher Education (2003, December 12). Characteristics of recipients of earned doctorates, 2002. A10.

Clark, R. (1971). *Einstein: The Life and times.* New York: The World Publishing Company.

Clifford, G.J. & Guthrie, J.W. (1988). *Ed School.* Chicago: University of Chicago Press.

Collins, J. (2001). *Good to great: Why some companies make the leap . . . and others don't.* New York: HarperCollins.

Collins, R. (1998). *The sociology of philosophies: A global theory of intellectual change.* Cambridge, MA: The Belknap Press of Harvard University Press.

Cowboy Way. (1998–2009). *Cowboy quotes, sayings, and wisdom.* Retrieved on June 9, 2009 from http://www.cowboyway.com/CowboyQuotes.htm.

Creighton, T. (2006). National Council of Professors of Educational Administration. In F. English (Ed.) *Encyclopedia of Educational Leadership and Administration* (pp. 691–2), Thousand Oaks, CA: SAGE.

Cremin, L. (1965). *The genius of American education.* Pittsburgh: University of Pittsburgh.

Crow, G. and Grogan, M. (2005).The development of leadership thought and practice in the United States. In F. English (Ed.) *The Sage handbook of educational leadership* (pp. 362–379). Thousand Oaks, CA: Sage.

Cuban, L. (1976). *Urban school chiefs under fire.* Chicago: University of Chicago Press.

Culbertson, J. (1995). *Building bridges: UCEA's first two decades.* University Park, PA: University Council for Educational Administration.

Culbertson, J. (1988). A century's quest for a knowledge base. In N. Boyan (Ed.) *Handbook of research on educational administration* (pp. 3–26). New York: Longman.

Cunningham, W. & Cordeiro, P. (2000). *Educational administration: A problem-based approach.* Boston: Allyn & Bacon.

DeMarrais, K. (2006). "The haves and the have mores"; Fueling a conservative ideological war on public education (or tracking the money). *Educational Studies, 39,* 201–240.

Deming, E. (1986). *Out of the crisis.* Cambridge: MIT Press.

Deming, E. (1993). *The new economics.* Cambridge, MA: MIT Press.

Devitt, M. & Sterelny, K. (1987). *Language and reality.* Cambridge: MIT Press.

Dewey, J. (1964-1904). The relation of theory to practice in education. In R. Archambault (Ed.) *John Dewey on education: Selected writings* (pp. 313–338). New York: The Modern Library.

Dewey, J. (1963). *Experience and education.* New York: Collier Books.

Dewey, J. (1929). *The sources of a science of education.* New York: Horace Liveright.

Dillon, S. (March 1, 2006). Online colleges receive a boost from congress. *The New York Times, CLV* (53,505), pp. A1–A17.

Donmoyer, R. (1999). The continuing quest for a knowledge base: 1976–1998. In J. Murphy & K. Seashore Louis, *Handbook of research on educational administration, 2nd ed.* (pp. 25–44). San Francisco, CA: Jossey-Bass.

Doscher, S. & Normore, A. (2008, January). The moral agency of the educational leader in times of national crisis and conflict. *Journal of School Leadership,* 18 (1), 8–31.

Dunham, B. (1964). *Heroes and heretics: A social history of dissent.* New York: Alfred A. Knopf.

Duke, D. (1989). The aesthetics of leadership. In J. Burdin (Ed.) *School leadership: A contemporary reader* (pp. 345–65) Newbury Park, CA: Sage.

Eisinger, P., & Hula, R. (2008). Gunslinger school administrators: Nontraditional leadership in urban school systems in the United States. In J. Munro (Ed.) *Educational Leadeship* (pp. 111–126). Boston, MA: McGraw-Hill.

Emanuel, E. (2006, October 20). How to redefine a medical education. *The Chronicle Review,* 43 (9), B12–13.

Emery, K. & Ohanian, S. (2004). *Why is corporate America bashing our public schools?* Portsmouth, NH: Heinemann.

English, F. (2009). The best of the best: The most influential international writing in educational administration in the last forty years. Introduction in F. English (Ed.) *Educational Leadership & Administration.* London, UK: Sage.

English, F. (2008). *Anatomy of professional practice: Promising research perspectives on educational leadership.* Lanham, MD: Rowman & Littlefield Education.

English, F. (2008b). *The art of educational leadership: Balancing performance and accountability.* Los Angeles, CA: Sage.

English, F. (2007). The NRC's scientific research in education: It isn't even wrong. In F. English and G. Furman (Eds.) *Research and educational leadership: Navigating the new National Research Council guidelines* (pp. 1–38). Lanham, MD: Rowman & Littlefield Education.

English, F. (2006, August). The unintended consequences of a standardized knowledge base in advancing educational leadership preparation. *Educational Administration Quarterly,* 42 (3), 461–472.

English, F. (2006b, August). Understanding leadership in education: Life writing and its possibilities. *Journal of Educational Administration and History,* 38 (2), 141–154.

English, F. (2004). Undoing the "done deal": Reductionism, ahistoricity, and pseudo-science in the knowledge base and standards for educational administration. *UCEA Review,* 46, 5–7.

English, F. (2004b). Learning "manifestospeak": A metadiscursive analysis of the Fordham Institute's and Broad Foundation's *Manifesto for Better Leaders for America's Schools.* In T. Lasley (Ed.) *Better leaders for America's schools: Perspectives on the Manifesto* (pp. 52–91. Columbia, MO: UCEA.

English, F. (2003, March). Cookie-cutter leaders for cookie-cutter schools: the teleology of standardization and the de-legitimization of the university in educational leadership preparation. *Leadership and Policy in Schools,* 2 (1), 27–46.

English, F. (2002). The fateful turn: Understanding the discursive practice of educational administration. In G. Perreault and F. Lunenburg (eds.) *The changing world of school administration* (pp.44–59), Lanham, MD: The Scarecrow Press.

English, F. (2000b). The point of scientificity, the fall of the epistemological dominos, and the end of the field of educational administration. *Studies in philosophy and education, 21*, 298–311.

English, F. (1998, September). Musings on Willower's "fog": A response. *Journal of School Leadership,* 8, 464–469.

English, F. (1997, January). The cupboard is bare: The postmodern critique of educational administration. *Journal of School Leadership,* 7 (1), 4–26.

English, F. (1995, May). Toward a reconsideration of biography and other forms of life writing as a focus for teaching educational administration. *Educational Administration Quarterly,* 31 (2), 203–223.

English, F. (1994). *Theory in educational administration.* New York: Harper Collins.

English, F. & Steffy, B. (1997, February). Using film to teach leadership in educational administration. *Educational Administration Quarterly,* 33 (1), 107–115.

Fairclough, N. (1992). *Discourse and social change.* Cambridge, UK: Polity Press.

Fenner, M. & Fishburn, E. (1944). *Pioneer American educators.* Washington, D.C. National Education Association.

Feyerabend, P. (1995). *Problems of empiricism, Vol. 2.* Cambridge: Cambridge University Press.

Feyerabend, P. (1993). *Against method.* London: Verso.

Finn, C. (1991). *We must take charge: Our schools and our future.* New York: The Free Press.

Foucault, M. (1980). In C. Gordon (Ed.). *Power/Knowledge.* New York: Pantheon Books.

Foucault, M. (1972). *The archaeology of knowledge.* New York: Pantheon Books.

Frank, P. (1949). Einstein's philosophy of science. *Reviews of Modern Physics,* 21 (3).

Fusarelli, L. (2006). University Council for Educational Administration. In F. English (Ed.) *Encyclopedia of Educational Leadership and Administration* (pp. 1044–5). Thousand Oaks, CA: Sage.

Gadet, F. (1986). *Saussure and contemporary culture.* London: Hutchinson Radius.

Gardner, J. (1991). *On leadership.* New York: Free Press.

Getzels, J. (1958). *Administration as a social process.* In A. Halpin (Ed.) Administrative theory in education. New York: The Macmillan Company.

Giroux, H. (2004). *The terror of neoliberalism: Authoritarianism and the eclipse of democracy.* Boulder, CA: Paradigm Publishers.

Gladwell, M. (2000). *The tipping point.* Little Brown Company.

Glass, T. (Ed.) (2004). *The history of educational administration viewed through its textbooks.* Lanham, MD: Scarecrow Education.

Grady, M. (2006). Cocking, Walter. In F. English (Ed.) *Encyclopedia of Educational Leadership and Administration* (pp. 157–8). Thousand Oaks, CA: SAGE.

Gratzer, W. (2002). *Eurekas and euphorias: The Oxford book of scientific anecdotes.* Oxford, UK: Oxford University Press.

Graves, R. (Trans.) (1979). *Gaius Suetonius Tranquillus: The twelve caesars.* New York. Penguin Books.

Greenfield, T.B. (1988). The decline and fall of science in educational administration, In D. Griffiths, R. Stout & P. Forsyth (Eds.) *Leaders for America's schools* (pp. 131–159). Berkeley, CA: McCutchan Publishing Corporation.

Greenfield, T.B. and Ribbins, P. (1993) (Eds.). *Greenfield on educational administration: Towards a humane science.* London: Routledge.

Gronn, P. (2003). *The new work of educational leaders: Changing leadership practice in an era of school reform.* London, UK: Paul Chapman.

Groopman, J. (2007) *How doctors think.* Boston. Houghton Mifflin Company.

Gunter, H. (2006, August). Knowledge production in the field of educational leadership: A place for intellectual histories" *Journal of Educational Administration and History,* 38 (2), 201–216.

Gunter, H. & Ribbins, P. (2002). Leadership studies in education: Towards a map of the field. *Educational Management and Administration,* 30 (4), 387–416.

Haack, S. (1978). *Philosophy of logics.* Cambridge, UK: Cambridge University Press.

Hall, E. (1981). *Beyond culture.* New York: Doubleday.

Haller, E. & Strike, K. (1986). *An introduction to educational administration: Social, legal, and ethical perspective.* New York: Longman.

Hanson, K. (2009). *A Casebook for school leaders: Linking the ISLLC standards to effective practice.* Columbus, Ohio: Pearson.

Hanson, E. (1991). *Educational administration and organizational behavior.* Boston: Allyn & Bacon.

Heilbrunn, J. (1996). Can leadership be studied? In P.S. Temes (Ed.) *Teaching leadership: Essays in theory and practice* (pp. 1–11). New York: Peter Lang.

Hess, F. (Ed.) (2008). *When research matters: How scholarship influences education policy.* Cambridge, MA: Harvard Education Press.

Hess, F. (2004). A license to lead? In T. Lasley (Ed.), *Better leaders for America's schools: Perspective on the Manifesto* (UCEA Monograph, pp. 36–51) Columbia, Missouri: UCEA.

Hess, F., & Kelly, A. (2005) Learning to lead? *Education Week,* 24, 37.

Hess, F. & Kelly, A. (2005b, March). An innovative look, a recalcitrant reality: The politics of principal preparation reform. *Educational Policy,* 19 (1), 155–180.

Hessel, K. & Holloway, J. (2002). *A framework for school leaders: Linking the ISLLC standards to practice.* Princeton, NJ: Educational Testing Service.

Higher Ed Inc. (September 10-16, 2005). Universities have become much more businesslike, but they are still doing the same old things. *The Economist, 376* (8443), 19–20.

Hills, R. (1969). *Toward a science of organization.* Eugene, Oregon: Center for the Advanced Study of Educational Administration: University of Oregon.

Hoffer, T.B., Welch, V., Williams, K., Hess, M., Webber, K., & Lisek, B. (2005). *Doctorate recipients from United States universities: Summary report 2004.* Chicago: National Opinion Research Center.

Hoy, W. & Miskel, C. (1982). *Educational administration: Theory, research, and practice.* New York: Random House.

Hoyle, J. (2006). Leadership, national standards. In F. English (Ed.) *Encyclopedia of educational leadership and administration* (pp. 568–571). Thousand Oaks, CA: SAGE.

Jaworksi, J. (1996). *Synchronicity: The inner path of leadership.* San Francisco: Berrett-Koehler Publishers.

Jelinek, M. (1979). *Institutionalizing innovation.* New York: Praeger.

Johnson, P. (1996). Antipodes: Plato, Nietzsche, and the moral dimensions of leadership. In P. Temes (Ed.) *Teaching Leadership: Essays in theory and practice* (pp. 13–44). New York: Peter Lang.

Johnson, S. (1998). *Who moved my cheese?* New York: G.P. Putnam & Sons.

Jung, C. (1958). *The undiscovered self.* R. Hull, trans. New York: Mentor Books.

Kamler, B. & Thomson, P. (2008, November). The failure of dissertation advice books: Toward alternative pedagogies for doctoral writing. *Educational Researcher,* 37 (8), 507–514.

Kanigel, R. (1997). *The one best way: Frederick Winslow Taylor and the enigma of efficiency.* New York: Viking.

Kendell, R. & Byrne, D. (1977, October). Thinking about the Greenfield-Griffiths debate *UCEA Review,* 19: 1, 6–16.

Khurana, R. (2002). *Searching for a corporate savior: The irrational quest for charismatic CEOs.* Princeton, N.J.: Princeton University Press.

Khurana, R. (2007). *From higher aims to hired hands: The social transformation of American business schools and the unfulfilled promise of management as a profession.* Princeton: Princeton University Press.

Kuhn, T. (1962). *The structure of scientific revolutions.* Chicago: University of Chicago Press.

Kowalski, T. (2004). The ongoing war for the soul of school administration, In T. Lasley (Ed.) *Better leaders for America's schools: Perspectives on the Manifesto* (pp. 92–114). Columbia, Missouri: UCEA.

Labaree, D.F. (2003, May). The peculiar problems of preparing educational researchers. *Educational Researcher,* 32 (4), 13–22.

Lakatos, I. (1999). *The methodology of scientific research programmes.* Cambridge, UK: Cambridge University Press.

Lakatos, I. (1999b). Lectures on scientific method. In M. Motterlini (Ed.) *For and against method.* Chicago: University of Chicago Press.

Lamberton, R. (2001). *Plutarch.* New Haven, CT: Yale University Press. Lather, P. (2009, May). History matters: Neoliberalism and the research/policy nexus. A book review. *Educational Researcher,* 38 (4), 284–289.

LeFanu, J. (1999). *The rise and fall of modern medicine.* New York: Carroll & Graf.

Leidecker, K. (1946). *Yankee teacher: The life of William Torrey Harris.* New York: The Philosophical Library.

Levin, H. (2006, November). Can research improve educational leadership? *Educational Researcher,* 35 (8): 38–43.

Levine, A. (2005). *Educating school leaders.* Washington, D.C. The Education Schools Project.

Lewontin, R. (1991). *Biology as ideology: The doctrine of DNA.* New York: HarperCollins.

Lieberman, D. (2001, November 19). Author: Data on successful firms 'faked' but still valid. *USA Today,* p. A.1.

Lopez, G. (2003). The (racially neutral) politics of education: a critical race theory perspective. *Educational Administration Quarterly,* 39 (1), 68–94.

Lumby, J. & English, F. (2009, April–June). From simplicism to complexity in leadership identity and preparation: exploring the lineage and dark secrets. *International Journal of Leadership in Education,* 12 (2), 95–114.

Lumby, J. & Coleman, M. (2007). *Leadership and diversity: Challenging theory and practice in education.* London: Sage.

Marshall, C. & Oliva, M. (2006). *Leadership for social justice: Making revolutions in education.* Boston: Pearson.

Maxcy, S. (2006). The metaphysical sources of a pragmatic aesthetic leadership. In E. Samier & R. Bates (Eds.) *Aesthetic dimensions of educational administration and leadership* (pp. 64–78). London: Routledge.

Maxcy, S. (1994). *Postmodern school leadership: Meeting the crisis in educational administration.* Westport, CT: Praeger.

Merton, R. (1968). *Social theory and social structure.* New York: The Free Press.

Milley, P. (2006). Aesthetic experience as resistance to the 'iron cage' of dominative administrative rationality. In E. Samier & R. Bates (Eds.), *Aesthetic dimensions of educational administration and leadership* (pp. 79–96) Oxon, UK: Routledge.

Miskel, C. (1988, October). *Research and the preparation of educational administrators.* Paper presented at the annual meeting of the University Council for Educational Administration, Cincinnati, Ohio.

Murphy, J. (2006). *Preparing school leaders: Defining a research and action agenda.* Lanham, MD: Rowman & Littlefield Education and UCEA.

Murphy, J. T. (March, 2006b). Dancing lessons for elephants: Reforming ed school leadership programs. *Phi Delta Kappan,* 87 (7), 489–491.

Murphy, J. (2005). Unpacking the foundations of ISLLC Standards and addressing the concerns in the academic community. *Educational Administration Quarterly,* 41 (1), 154–191.

Murphy, J. (2000, October–November) A response to English. *International Journal of Leadership in Education* 3 (4), 399–410.

Murphy, J. (1999). *The quest for a center: Notes on the state of the profession of educational leadership.* Columbia, MO: UCEA.

Murphy, J. & Vriesenga, M. (2004). *Research on preparation programs in educational administration: An analysis.* Tempe, Arizona: UCEA.

Murphy, J., Vresenga, M. & Storey, V. (2007, December). Educational administration quarterly, 1979–2003: An analysis of types of work, methods of investigation, and influences, *Educational Administration Quarterly,* 43 (5), 612–628.

Murphy, J., Yff, J. & Shipman, N. (2000, January–March), Implementation of the inter-state school leaders licensure consortium standards, 3 (1), 17–40.

National Commission on Excellence in Educational Administration. (1987). *Leaders for American schools: The report of the national commission on excellence in educational administration.* Tempe, Arizona: UCEA.

National Opinion Research Center (2002).Characteristics of recipients of earned doctorates, 2002. *The Chronicle of Higher Education* (2003, December 12), A10.

National Research Council (NRC) Committee Scientific Principles for Education Research (2002). *Scientific research in education.* R.J. Shavelson & L. Towne (Eds.). Washington, DC: National Academy Press.

O'Conner, A. (2007). *Social science for what? Philanthropy and the social question in a world turned rightside up.* New York: Russell Sage Foundation.

Owen, R. (1987). *Organizational behavior in education.* Englewood Cliffs, NJ: Prentice-Hall.

Owings, W. & Kaplan, L. (Eds.) (2003). *Best practices, best thinking and emerging issues in school leadership.* Thousand Oaks, CA: Corwin Press.

Papa, R. (2004). Practice of theory to theory of practice: The prime directive. *The Eighth Yearbook of the National Council of Professors of Educational Administration.* Lancaster: Economic Publishing Co., Inc.

Papa, R. (2008). *Leadership on the frontlines: Changes in preparation and practice.* NCPEA Yearbook. Papa, R. (Editor); Achilles, C.M. and Alford, B. (Assoc. Editors), August, 2008. DEStech Publications, Inc. Lancaster, PA.

Papa, R. & Brown, R. (2007). On the founding of joint and independent doctoral programs. In *The Handbook of Doctoral Programs in Educational Administration: Issues and Challenges.* NCPEA Connexions e-book. Retrieved on January 10, 2009 from www.connexions.soe.vt.edu/docbook.html.

Papa, R. & English, F. (2009). A critical review of trends in dissertation research in educational leadership 2006-08. Unpublished paper.

Parsons, T. (1951). *The social system.* New York: The Free Press.

Pattison, S. (1997). *The faith of the managers: When management becomes religion.* London: Cassell.

Peters, T. & Waterman, R. (1982). *In search of excellence: Lessons from America's best-run companies.* New York: Harper & Row.

Peirce, C. (1934–1948). *Collected papers* (4 vols.) Cambridge, MA: Harvard University Press.

Peirce, C. (1955). *Philosophical writings of Peirce.* J. Buchler (Ed.).New York: Dover.

Porter, R. (1999). *The greatest benefit to mankind: A medical history of humanity.* New York: W.W. Norton.

ProQuest. (2009). *Educational leadership dissertations.* Retrieved on October 17, 2008; December 1, 2008 and January 6, 2009 from: http://proquest.umi.com/pqdweb?SQ=Educational+Leadership+Dissertations

Quote DB. (2009). *Albert Einstein.* Retrieved on June 8, 2009 from http://www.quotedb.com/quotes/2310.

Razik, T. & Swanson, A. (2010). *Fundamental concepts of educational leadership & management.* Boston, MA: Allyn and Bacon.

Ribbins, P. (2006). Aesthetics and art: Their place in the theory and practice of leadership in education. In E. Samier and R. Bates (Eds.) *Aesthetic Dimensions of Educational Administration and Leadership* (pp. 175–190). Oxon, UK: Routledge.

Riehl, C., Larson, C., Short, P.M., Reitzug, U.C. (2000, August). Reconceptualizing research and scholarship in educational administration: Learning to know, knowing to do, doing to learn. *Educational Administration Quarterly,* 36 (3), 391–399.

Rousmaniere, K. (2005). *Citizen teacher: The life and leadership of Margaret Haley.* Albany, NY: State University of New York Press.

Rost, J. (1991). *Leadership for the Twenty-First Century.* New York: Praeger.

Saltman, K. (2005). *The Edison schools: Corporate schooling and the assault on public education.* New York:Routledge.

Samier, E. (2005). Towards public administration as a humanities discipline: A humanistic manifesto. *Halduskultuur: Administrative Culture,* 6, 6–59.

Samier, E. & Atkins, T. (2009). The problem of narcissists in positions of power: the grandiose, the callous, and the irresponsible in educational administration and leadership. In E. Samier & M. Schmidt (Eds.) (pp. 212–223), Oxon, UK: Routledge.

Seashore Louis, K. & Honig, M. (2007, February). A new agenda for research in educational leadership: A conversational review. *Educational Administration Quarterly* 43 (1): 138–48.

Schaefer, R. (1990). Footnotes on Callahan's teachers college. In W. Eaton (Ed.) *Shaping the Superintendency: A Reexamination of Callahan and the Cult of Efficiency.* New York: Teachers College Press.

Shen, J. (1999). *The school of education: its mission, faculty, and reward structure.* New York: Peter Lang.

Shipman, N. (2006). Interstate school leaders licensure consortium. In F. English (Ed.) *Encyclopedia of educational leadership and administration* (pp. 524–6). Thousand Oaks, CA: SAGE.

Shipman, N., Queen, J. & Peel, H. (2007). *Transforming school leadership with ISLLC and ELCC.* Larchmont, NY: Eye on Education.

Shoho, A., Merchant, B. & Lugg, C. (2005). Social justice: Seeking a common language. In F. English (Ed.), *The SAGE handbook of educational leadership: Advances in theory, research, and practice,* (pp. 47–67). Thousand Oaks, CA: SAGE.

Shulman, L. S., Golde, C.M., Bueschel, A.C., & Garabedian, K.J. (2006, April). Reclaiming education's doctorates: A critique and a proposal. *Educational Researcher,* 35 (3), 25–32.

Simon, H. (1947). *Administrative Behavior.* New York: The Free Press.

Sontag, S. (1978). *On photography.* New York: Farrar, Straus and Giroux.

Spiegel, P. (2009, June 12). Commander maps new course in Afghan war," *The Wall Street Journal,* 253 (136), A6.

Starratt, R. (1993). *The drama of leadership.* London: Falmer Press.

Taylor, F. (1967/1911). *The principles of scientific management.* New York: W.W. Norton.

Temes, P. (1996). Teaching leadership/Teaching ethics: Martin Luther King's "letter from Birmingham jail" In P. Temes (Ed.) *Teaching leadership: Essays in theory and practice* (pp. 73–82). New York: Peter Lang.

The Quotations Page. *Charles H. Duell.* Retrieved on June 1, 2009 from http://www. quotationspage.com/quotes/Charles H. Duell.

Tice, G. (1977) as cited in S. Sontag (1977) *On photography.* New York: Farrar, Straus and Giroux.

The Chronicle. (2008, August 29). Degrees awarded by type of institution, 2005–2006. *The Chronicle of Higher Education: Almanac Issue 2008–09, LV* (1), 20.

The Quotations Page. (1994-2007). *Louis Pasteur* (1822–1895). Retrieved on January 18, 2009 from http://www.quotationspage.com/quotes/Louis_Pasteur/.

Thomas, G. (1997). What's the use of theory? *Harvard Educational Review,* 67 (1), 75–104 as cited in Riehl, Larson, Short & Reitzug (2000, p. 394).

Thompson, J. (1967). *Organizations in action: Social science bases of administrative theory.* New York: McGraw-Hill Book Company.

Tillman, L. (2003). From rhetoric to reality: Educational administration and the lack of racial and ethnic diversity within the profession. *UCEA Review,* 45 (3): 1–4.

Tillman, L. (2002). Culturally sensitive research approaches: An African American perspective. *Educational Researcher,* 31 (9): 3–12.

Turner, C. (1990). *Organizational culture.* Mendip Paper 007. Blagdon, UK: The Staff College.

Usher, R. & Edwards, R. (1996). *Postmodernism and education.* London, UK: Routledge.

Warren, R. (2002). *The purpose driven life.* Grand Rapids, Michigan: Zondervan. Watt, J. (1994). Ideology, objectivity, and education. New York: Teachers College Press.

Watt, J. (1994). *Ideology, objectivity, and education.* New York: Teachers College Press.

West, C. (1999). Race and modernity. In C. West (Ed.) *The Cornell West reader* (pp. 55–86). New York: Basic Civatis Books.

Weber, M. (1968). *Economy and society: An outline of interpretive sociology.* New York: Bedminster Press.

Whittemore, R. (1988). *Pure Lives: The early biographers.* Baltimore, MD: The Johns Hopkins University Press.

Wiens, J. (2006). Educational leadership as civic humanism. In P. Kelleher and R. Van Der Bogert (Eds.), V*oices for democracy: Struggles and celebrations of transforming leaders,* 199–225. Malden, MA: Blackwell.

Williams, W. (2005, September 9). Ineligible research. *The Chronicle Review,* 42 (3), B24. Willis, E. (2005, September 9). The pernicious concept of 'balance'. *The Chronicle Review*, 42 (3) B11.

Willower, D. (1998). Fighting the fog: A criticism of postmodernism. *Journal of School Leadership* 8 (5), 444–463.

Willower, D. (1994). *Educational administration: Inquiry, values, practice.* Lancaster, PA: Technomic.

Wood, L. (1984). Behaviorism. In D. Runes (Ed.). *Dictionary of philosophy.* Totowa, NJ: Rowman & Allanheld, 50–1.

Woods, P. (2005). *Democratic leadership in education.* London, UK: Paul Chapman.

Young, M. and Lopez, G. (2005). The nature of inquiry in educational leadership. In F. English (Ed.). *The SAGE handbook of educational leadership* (pp. 337-61). Thousand Oaks, CA: SAGE.

Subject Index

Author Index

About the Authors

A brief sketch of the authors of *Restoring Human Agency to Educational Administration: Status and Strategies.*

FENWICK W. ENGLISH

Terminal Degree:
Ph.D. Arizona State University, 1972

Current Position:
The R. Wendell Eaves Senior Distinguished Professor in Educational Leadership, University of North Carolina at Chapel Hill since 2001

K–12 Teaching Experience:
Elementary and middle school, Southern California 1961–64

K–12 Administrative Experience:
Middle School Principal, Temple City, CA; Assistant Superintendent of Schools, Sarasota, Florida; Superintendent of Schools, New York 1965–1977

Association Experience:
Associate Executive Director, AASA 1977–79

Private Sector Experience:
Partner, National Education Practice Director, Peat, Marwick, Mitchell & Co., Washington, D.C. 1979–1982

Professorships:
Lehigh University; University of Cincinnati; University of Kentucky; Indiana-Purdue University, Ft. Wayne, IN; Iowa State University; University of North Carolina at Chapel Hill 1984–2009

Higher Education Administrative Experience:
Department Chair, University of Cincinnati; Dean, School of Education, Indiana-Purdue University, Fort Wayne, IN: Vice-Chancellor of Academic Affairs, Indiana-Purdue University, Fort Wayne, IN: Interim Dean, UNC-Chapel Hill 1987–2003

Doctoral Program Innovation:
Member, University of Kentucky when participating in the Danforth Program to redefine educational leadership programs 1991–95

Professional Association Leadership:
UCEA Executive Committee, 2001–09
UCEA President, 2006–07

Refereed Papers Presented Nationally/Internationally:
NCPEA, UCEA, AERA, BELMAS (British Educational Leadership and Management Association Society)

Editorships:
SAGE Handbook of Educational Leadership, 2005
SAGE Encyclopedia of Educational Leadership, 2006
SAGE Library of Educational Thought and Practice, 2009

Walter Cocking Invitational Lecture:
NCPEA, San Antonio, Texas 2009

Founding Journal Editor:
International Journal of Educational Reform 1992–2000;

Outstanding Consultancies:
Chicago School Finance Authority, 1990–94
Tennessee Academy of School Leaders, 1993
Georgia State Board of Education, 2002
Albertson Foundation, Boise, Idaho, 1998

Refereed Journal Publications:
Educational Researcher
Education Administration Quarterly
Journal of Educational Administration & History
Journal of School Leadership
International Journal of Leadership in Education

Recently Published Books:
The Art of Educational Leadership, SAGE, 2008
Anatomy of Professional Practice, Rowman and Littlefield Education, 2008
The Postmodern Challenge to the Theory and Practice of Educational Administration, Charles Thomas, 2003

ROSEMARY PAPA

Terminal Degree:
Ed.D. University of Nebraska-Lincoln, 1983

Current Position:
The Del and Jewell Lewis Endowed Chair for Educational Leadership, Northern Arizona University since 2007

K–12 Teaching Experience:
Elementary and junior high school, Southern California 1972–77;

K–12 Administrative Experience:
Chief School Administrator and Principal, K–8 Catholic school and K–12 Catholic district in Bellevue and Omaha, Nebraska 1978–1985

Association Experience:
Member, National Policy Board for Educational Administration, 1991–92

Private Sector Experience:
Regional Vice President, Business Division, Sylvan Learning Systems 1998–2000

Professorships:
University of New Orleans, California State University, Fresno; California State University, Sacramento; Northern Arizona University 1985–2009

Higher Education Administrative Experience:
Assistant Vice Chancellor, Academic Affairs, Inter-Institutional Relations with the University of California, Chancellor's Office, California State University System; Director, Center for Teaching and Learning, California State University, Sacramento 1995–2007

Doctoral Program Innovation:
Founding CSU Director, Joint Doctoral Program, Cal State Fresno and UC System (UCLA, UCR, UCSB, UCD and UCSC; Founding Director, Capital Area North Doctorate in Educational Leadership; 1986–2007

Professional Association Leadership:
APEA President Arizona Professors of Education Administration, 2008–2010; AZ School Administrators, Higher Ed Div., President-Elect, 2008–2010 NCPEA Executive Board, 1990–93; NCPEA President, 1991–92; President, California Professors of Educational Administration, 1989 and 1990

Refereed Papers Presented Nationally/Internationally:
NCPEA, UCEA, AERA, International School Leaders, Uppsala, Sweden; Colloquium, University of Sydney, Australia; Peking University, Beijing, China; Cote d''Ivoire Higher Education African Conference; N.I.I.E.D., Republic of Korea Seminar for Educators

Editorships:
Greenwood Dictionary of Education: Administration, Management & Policy 2010
SAGE Library of Educational Thought and Practice, 2009
NCPEA Yearbooks 2008 and 2007

Walter Cocking Invitational Lecture:
NCPEA, 1999, Jackson Hole, Wyoming

Living Legend Award:
NCPEA, 2003, Sedona Arizona

Founding Journal Editor:
Journal on Education Policy 2000–present

Outstanding Consultancies:
Macmillan McGraw-Hill mathematics, social studies, ELL and reading 2004–2009; Scholastic reading 2001–2006; Pearson teacher technology, 2001–2006; Chair, I-Homework, org Board, 2000–01; Vice-Chair, California Student Aid Commission, 1998–2000; Chair, Ed Fund Board, 1999–2000

Refereed Journal Publications:
Education Leadership Review
Reading Improvement
The International Journal of Educational Management
Planning and Changing
The Journal of School Business Management

Recently Published Books:
Technology for School Improvement Sage, 2010
So You Want to Be a Higher Education Administration? Avoid Crossing to the Dark Side or What They Don't Teach in Summer Institutes. ProActive Publications with R. Brown and P. Noble, 2009
Leadership on purpose: Promising Practices with African American and Hispanic Students. Corwin With R. Fortune (2002)